PRAISE FOR
TWO BIPOLAR CHICKS GUIDE TO SURVIVAL

"I don't know any psychologists or M.D.s, including myself, who could have written this book by the Two Bipolar Chicks. I can't tell you how ecstatic I am. These Chicks have come up with every rule to save your life as you know it. Listen to what they say. The first thing I asked Wendy after I read the book is, 'Can I send this to my daughter . . . right now!?'"

—DR. JAY CARTER,
internationally best-selling author of five books,
including *The Complete Idiot's Guide to Bipolar Disorder*

"This is an incredible resource and edgy self-help guide about bipolar disorder which will soften the blow of the diagnosis, teach you how to cope and manage with the illness and help you navigate on a daily basis. This book is a must-read because it will save lives."

—ANDY BEHRMAN,
author of *Electroboy: A Memoir of Mania*

"*Two Bipolar Chicks Guide to Survival: Tips for Living with Bipolar Disorder* is a must read for consumers and caregivers alike. Their 66 straight forward tips cover the topics and issues most pertinent to coping and managing bipolar disorder. Wendy and Honora offer a realistic and compassionate glimpse into their lives, giving the reader survival rules, hope, and encouragement."

—MUFFY WALKER MSN,
MBA founder & Chairman of International Bipolar Foundation,
a psychiatric nurse and mother to a son with bipolar.

"*Two Bipolar Chicks Guide to Survival: Tips for Living with Bipolar Disorder* is an excellent survival guide for navigating the complexities of the mental health care system. It is a unique self-help book that approaches the management of bipolar illness with a very practical approach. I especially recommend this book for patients, families, as well as 'bipolar chicks.'"

—ROBERT C. BRANSFIELD, M.D., DLFAPA
Clinical Associate Professor of Psychiatry,
Rutgers-Robert Wood Johnson Medical School,
Past President, New Jersey Psychiatric Association

"Two Bipolar Chicks' straight forward approach to bipolar disorder is not only enlightening and refreshing, but encouraging! Compassionately, yet candidly, their knowledge and experience of bipolar disorder is clearly conveyed. Williamson and Rose's no-nonsense guide expertly steers you through bipolar disorder from pill boxes, to manic sex, all the way to learning to find acceptance of the illness. More than a decade after my own diagnosis, I find these clear-cut tips are relevant and exactly what every bipolar person needs."

—MRS. BIPOLARITY

"In the late 1980's, Dr. Ronald R. Fieve gave us *Moodswing* (Bantam Press, NYC, 1989). His work is still considered seminal in pioneering the utilization of lithium to treat manic depression. In the 90's, Dr. Kay Redfield Jamison of John Hopkins blew the doors open when she self-disclosed her Manic Depressive and removed the stigma for millions of Americans with the publication of *An Unquiet Mind: A Memoir of Moods and Madness* (Alfred Knopf, NYC, 1995). The first decade of the new millennium brought us more scholarly and self-help books on bipolar illness than the past fifty years. Now we have

Two Bipolar Chicks Guide to Survival: Tips for Living with Bipolar Disorder: a thorough, well researched, systematic and enjoyable resource for individuals and family members and friends trying to understand, live with, cope with, recover from, heal and thrive with the disease of bipolar illness. Professionals of all disciplines will be thrilled to have their work as a resource."

—LAURA MADLYN HARRISON, MA, LCADC, CLEM

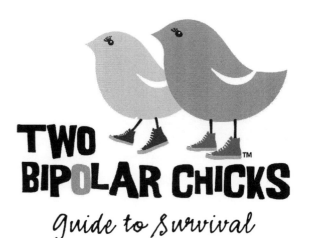

TWO BIPOLAR CHICKS™

Guide to Survival

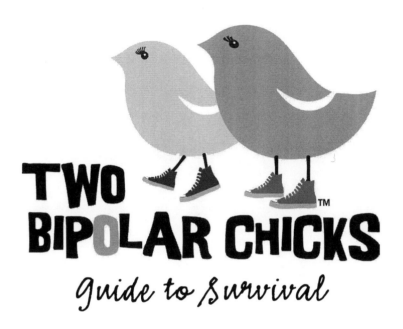

TWO BIPOLAR CHICKS™

Guide to Survival

• Tips for Living with Bipolar Disorder •

· · · · · · · · · · · · · · · · · · ·

WENDY K. WILLIAMSON and HONORA ROSE

Post Hill PRESS

WENDY

. . . .

For Parker, Katie, Seamus, Megan and Devin,

When I'm not around, know that I am hunkered at my desk writing, wishing I could spend more time with you. If only I could have it both ways. You complete our family with style and spunk and I love you madly.

To my parents,

What you have done for me can never be measured or summed up in a few sentences. You have no idea what your love and support over the years has done in keeping me alive and feeling loved. You've also taught me the value in hard work and perseverance which has come in handy. And mom, I owe you a special thanks for your willingness to read even the roughest of drafts with your cheerful attitude and red teacher's pen. You've always made a fantastic first editor.

. . . .

HONORA

. . . .

To my mom and dad,

You never gave up on me even when I gave up on myself. Many dark days you were there to assure me that everything would be okay. And you were always right. Your faith in me never wavered; you told me I could do anything I put my mind to. It is for that reason I am still here—doing well, happy, healthy and loving a life that a few years ago I could have only dreamt. Thank you for believing in me. I love you very much.

To John Henry and Eleanor,

The two brightest and happiest days of my life were the days each of you were born. You were, and always will be, shining stars in my heart and soul. John Henry, in you I see my fearlessness and determination. And Ellie, in you, my artistic free spirit. I wish for you to find what makes you happy. Life is too short for "should haves" or "would haves". I love you both with all my heart. You are the best thing that ever happened to me and one day we will be together again.

ACKNOWLEDGEMENTS

We know this book wouldn't have seen the light of day without our dynamic, super cool agent, Corinda. She knows the dreams business and we are proud to be part of her world. A huge thank you goes out to Anthony and Michael at Post Hill Press who took a chance on a couple of bipolar chicks at the inception of their company. Thank you to our editor Emilia for your precision and flow, and to the entire staff at Post Hill Press who added time and care to our book.

A huge thank you goes out to Kim Sillen for her endless talents, devotion and willingness to drop her work on a dime for us. The best part of being able to work with you is staying close to our lifelong friendship that started with Izod shirts, tube socks and trips to Hilton Head.

Thank you God for giving us each other, the goofiest bipolar chicks we know. You knew we needed laughter and constant hijinks in order to maintain any semblance of sanity. And we love you for that.

CONTENTS

CHAPTER 7
CREATE YOUR LIFE 93

CHAPTER 8
ORGANIZATION IS THE KEY TO SUCCESS 105

CHAPTER 9
SUNSHINE 119

CHAPTER 14
THE END   187

FOREWORD

Hats Off to the Bipolar Chicks

by Dr. Jay Carter, Psy.D.

International Best-selling author including
The Complete Idiot's Guide to Bipolar Disorder

I don't know any psychologists or M.D.s, including myself, who could have written this book by the Two Bipolar Chicks. Over the past nine years I have given trainings in bipolar disorder for over thirty thousand mental health professionals. At every training I have stated that the missing link between the science and treatment of bipolar disorder is . . . the practicalities.

My mother had bipolar disorder (BiPD), so I was raised by someone with BiPD, and one of my daughters has BiPD, so I raised someone with BiPD. If this book was available, it would have made life 1,000% better for my mother, daughter, and myself. I have written five international books, including one best seller. But to be honest, I don't enjoy writing books. It's just something I felt led to do. I can't tell you how ecstatic I am that Wendy K. Williamson, BiPD and Honora A. Rose, BiPD have written this book.

The Two Bipolar Chicks have asked me to write about scientific phenomena, so I am going to give you the most significant phenomenological information I have found thus far, backed up with brain scan activity and latest research on executive functions.

The most noted discovery that I have found in people with BiPD is the loss of executive function during mania. That would be the loss of insight, foresight, hindsight, and lack of ability to "see" the consequences of their actions. My best phrase for this is that they are not "seeing themselves." A mere intellectual understanding of the consequences is not real without vision. When a person is manic, they may be thinking six times faster than you. They may get impatient with you for talking so slowly. They are brilliant. Don't argue with them: they will win. But they lack the ability to "see" the consequences of their actions, or the context of the situation. The prefrontal lobe is that part of us that enables us to see ourselves. No other mammal on earth has this ability.

During mania there is a flood of activity in the prefrontal lobe. Racing thoughts knock out the ability to see the bigger picture of things with overwhelming details. Then after the mania, there is a distinct lack of activity in the prefrontal lobe for up to six to eight weeks afterward. This is diagnosed as "lack of insight" in most analyses, but a better term would be a temporary lack of executive functions.

The prefrontal lobe executive functions are subtle. It is the last thing that develops in the brain and it is the first thing to go. When you lose it, you don't know you lost it. I have never heard of anyone saying to their therapist, "You know, I think I lost my prefrontal lobe in that last manic episode, because I am not seeing the big picture of things, and I have no insight, foresight, or hindsight." Because . . . if they could say THAT, their prefrontal lobe would be working! (You can see more on this at my free one and a half hour seminar at: bipolarlight. com or by searching "midwestpictures" on You Tube.)

Another important thing about BiPD is how it affects relationships. When our prefrontal lobe is online, we "see" what we are thinking and decide whether we are going to say it or not. So, you might think your boss or your spouse is a jerk, but after you weigh it out, you may decide not to say it for the sake of the relationship. When a person is manic, the brain is directly connected to the tongue. There is a lack prefrontal lobe filtering things out. We all have private thoughts, but when manic, whatever we are thinking may roll off the tip of our tongues. The person we are saying these things to may take it personally. Again, this phenomenon is directly related to lack of executive function in the prefrontal lobe, as well as job loss for "insubordination."

When the prefrontal lobe goes out like a light bulb, a person may run up their credit cards or have unprotected sex without envisioning the consequences. We know the elderly often need help with taking their medication. This, again, relates to the lack of prefrontal lobe online. The same with bipolar (temporarily) and the authors have brilliant solutions. The Two Bipolar Chicks have nailed the most important and most successful aspect of battling BiPD. . . ensuring you take your meds.

When the lobe goes off line, what's the next best thing to a lobe? Rules. Procedures. Children have no lobe. They need rules, no matter how brilliant they are. They need rules like "Don't walk down dark alleys." "Don't get in a car with a stranger." An adult without a functioning prefrontal lobe is like a brilliant kid.

These Chicks have come up with every rule to save your life as you know it. Listen to what they say. Their prefrontal lobes were online and panoramic when they wrote this book. The first thing I asked Wendy after I read the book is, "Can I send this to my daughter . . . right now!?"

Dr. Jay Carter
jaycarter.net
bipolarlight.com

INTRODUCTION

After writing my first book, *I'm Not Crazy Just Bipolar*, I received a lot of feedback. Specifically, you wanted to know more about wellness and how I maintain it. You knew the basics: take your medication, see your professionals. You knew that music makes you feel better and being honest gets you further than hiding from the truth. Yet there were blanks that needed filling in and your loved ones also asked: What more can we do to help our beloved bipolar? I decided to answer you collectively and thus *Two Bipolar Chicks Guide to Survival: Tips for Living with Bipolar Disorder* was born.

Although I touched on the main topics in *I'm Not Crazy Just Bipolar*, I have since compiled a larger, more comprehensive list. I racked my brain to include and describe every single thing I could think of. In addition, I enlisted the help of my partner and editor, Honora Rose, who also has bipolar disorder, without whom this list would be incomplete. Together, we have put our bipolar minds together and brainstormed every itty, bitty thing we do to say what we think you need to know—if you don't already. It's a list we wish we knew about years ago when we first got diagnosed.

Have no fear: wellness is attainable if it isn't already at your doorstep. Follow a few simple, but not always easy, tips and tricks, and you will find yourself on your way. Nothing can cure our illness, but we do believe the more of these you practice, the greater the chance you'll spend less time in mania or depression. We have. In the least, perhaps you will have a few new tips on how to fine tune this illness while you're at sea level.

True, we are not doctors, nor do we have any initials after our names. But we are experts in living with bipolar disorder. It is our wish that something inside these pages will assist you in leading a more balanced and enjoyable life.

Some of these are very basic and some are more complex, but we swear by them all. We sincerely hope you find our collective experiences useful and that you are able to integrate them into your lives as well.

In love and health,
Wendy & Honora

In this book, since we both have bipolar disorder type I, we will be speaking from this perspective. We tried to keep it general to avoid excluding anyone from the club.

For more information on the various types and differences, refer to sites:

www.nimh.nih.org, www.nami.org, www.dbsa.org
or www.internationalbipolarfoundation.org.

This book is dedicated to:

You

Chapter 1

WHAT A PILL

Tip One: The Trusty Pill Tray

This tip has several parts to it. Number one, we suggest you use a pill tray. They're handy, they're cheap and they keep us organized. With the number of meds most bipolars take, we can use any help we can get! Juggling bottles is a drag and can get confusing. With one memory slip, which happens, it's way too easy to miss a dose. The pill tray is the simplest solution. It's Bipolar 101. Use a pill tray. If you don't have one, we suggest you: run—don't walk—and get yourself a locking pill tray. You'll save yourself some serious aggravation. Keeping track of our mini-pharmacies isn't easy, but it can be more convenient using a tray.

Personally, we don't always remember what day it is, let alone if we took our meds that morning. Without our pill trays I don't know where we'd be. Thank God there is a compartment to refer back to. Did I take my a.m. meds? Is there an empty chamber? Why yes, there is. Cool, I did take my a.m. meds. Easy breezy thank you, Mr. Pill Tray. It's a no brainer and that's why it falls under Bipolar 101. Without our beloved trays, there could be potentially severe consequences for us. We all know what those are, so we won't spell them out here.

Number two, we strongly urge you to get pill trays with the locking compartments. The package should say "locking" or childproof or something of the sort. Typically, there is a white tab that sticks out on the end. Trust us, you will have numerous pill explosions until you catch on and get one of these helpful numbers.

PILL TRAY ADVICE:

♦ Buy one that locks to avoid explosions.

♦ Beware of pharmacy freebies —they don't usually lock.

♦ Match the number of compartments to your dose frequency.

♦ Get one that works for your lifestyle.

♦ Try www.forgettingthepill.com for variations.

♦ Get more mileage: sharpie the days back on when they wear off!

Number three, get the pill tray that works for you. If you don't, you are apt to ditch it altogether. Obviously if pill trays were in a beauty contest, they would all tie for last. While there are no attractive styles, there are enough types; they range from simple to the complex. Often the simpler and cheaper trays suffice. If you want to get fancy, there are the spaceship looking ones that have timers and rotating devices. They're more expensive though. Spaceships cost money to make. We have created makeshift trays for free by using timers on our cell phones, set twice a day, so we don't forget to take meds from our simple a.m./p.m. locking ones. Looking at those spaceship types give us anxiety. Can you imagine mistakes and malfunctioning? What if you couldn't get it open? See? Anxiety already. They probably work like a charm for some. If you are on the go, though, having an ugly, portable, plastic tray is handy. Part of the aversion to pill trays is the hideous, unfashionable style. We understand. We've been there. We're still there. Someone needs to put some style in to these things. The ones in the pharmacy are limited but work.

> One of us—who shall go nameless—when in a manic state, wanted to start a company to make stylish pill boxes. (Needless to say it didn't happen!)
>
> •
>
> Curious to know who it was?
> Keep reading!
> The answer will be revealed.

If you are looking for what works for you, we combed a few websites and found a large, varied selection on www.forgettingthepill.com. In fact, they have every type of tray! Who knew there were so many? They have everything from travel trays with cases to entire month organizers in mini-plastic drawer types. They have containers on key chains and pills hidden away in mirrors with funny sayings and pictures on them. There are the spaceship ones we mentioned with the electronic timers. It will depend upon your preference, lifestyle and price range. The main thing is that you take your meds and find what works for you. If you're a business person, we realize you're not going to carry you're gigantic, rainbow, four-times-a-day pill tray around. We get it. Choose what you will use.

 WENDY:

I have my pills crammed into the once-a-day, one week, safety-latched pill tray. It fits easily into my purse so I can always have it with me. My first one was a freebie from the pharmacy and it was a disaster! I had constant purse explosion situations to clean up. It was such a drag. It kept happening until I finally heard about the safety latches. What a tip! I should use a twice a day one, but I know I wouldn't carry that around.

 HONORA:

In 2009, I got into a very serious car accident. I had my huge, ugly, three-times-a-day, rainbow, (non-locking) pill tray on the passenger's seat along with my purse. When I was broadsided, it slammed into the dashboard. Pills of every shape and color lay at my feet and all over the inside of my car. It looked like an earthquake hit a pharmacy counter. Of course when the police arrived, I had a lot of explaining to do. (Thank God I always carry with me my psychiatrist's name and signature on his prescription blank; they backed off.) The lesson I learned? Get the pill trays with safety latches; they make them for a reason. It's the first thing I looked for before I bought a new one.

Tip Two: Don't Leave Home Without It

Those old American Express commercials ring true. You never know when you'll need your trusty pill tray, so bring it along with you. There's nothing like having your constant companion rattling with the rhythm of your walk. No one likes the idea of keeping them glued to their side 24/7. But you never know when you will be stuck out and can't get to your tray in time. It's best to think like a girl or boy scout: always be prepared.

SO YOU DON'T LEAVE HOME WITHOUT IT:

1. Keep it in your purse or by your keys to remember it. Out of sight, out of mind.
2. Experiment! Find the pill tray that works for you and your lifestyle.
3. Try pop-outs if you dislike carrying bulky weekly trays.
4. Before leaving, ask yourself: Do I have my keys? Do I have my meds? Am I locking the door?

Still, they are hardly a box of candy and who among us is thrilled to be associated with them? Especially in our twenties, their annoying, little rattle made us feel like senior citizens. It reminds us we have an illness. "Hear me rattle, hear me roar!" Their jiggle may cause the occasional second glance. (Or is that our own paranoia?) The good news is pill trays can fit easily in to our purses. Fellas, it will fit in to your backpacks or man purse. Don't have a man purse or backpack? Okay, try bringing one of those daily pop-outs and put them in your outfit for the day. Or, there is always the discreet, barrel keychain option. You can tell any nosy nellie who asks, if they ask, you take a boatload of vitamins and you take them all throughout the day. Can't be without your healthy vitamins. Do they take them? They will forget all about your little hideaway.

While the pill box market is far from stylish or as varied as jeans, there are options to accommodate different strategies and types that will ensure you take 'em along. You can keep the larger ones in your glove box or at home. (There are rules with law enforcement about medication in the car. Check your state. We keep our psychiatrist and psychologist cards on us but our law goes beyond that.)

Emergencies without our meds have taught us to keep them on us. Storms have come and gone, family emergencies, car accidents and through it all, we've learned our lessons the hard way. Now, we are virtually velcroed to our pill trays and they are never more than twenty feet from our bodies. Think of it like a teddy bear to a child, except children have their bears closer. We're not *that* bad; we allow some distance. But we always know where they are.

 **WENDY:**

I used to be one of those people who hated to keep my pills on me unless absolutely necessary. I never had them in my purse. I took them before work and left them at home to take afterwards. In my early to mid-twenties, I don't remember even taking my meds all of the time. No need to worry about trays! One night changed my mind.

About seventeen years ago on Thanksgiving, I left my pill tray at home. My sister was hosting dinner five minutes away. No sense in bringing the pill tray, right? I would be home for p.m. meds in plenty of time.

We got a distress call from my uncle who had become disoriented, one hour away and I was the only one who knew exactly where he was. We picked him up and rushed to Sloan Kettering in New York City. We had no idea we'd stay there overnight, but there we were. My headache grew and pill tray lay waiting for me back home in New Jersey. The next day, my mom had to make a special trip to the city just to bring me my meds. After that night, I have never, ever, gone anywhere without them. Not even to the beach. When Hurricane

Sandy came to town, we were given mandatory evacuation. You better believe the first thing I packed was my pill bag and tray. I literally don't leave home without it.

Tip Three: The Ziploc

What better way to keep all of your medications together than in a Ziploc? Sure, there might be fancier bags—and we've tried them—but the Ziploc makes the most sense to us. They are cheap, see-through and easy to open and close. Plus if you travel, they fit conveniently in to any space. We are huge fans of the Ziplocs; it sure beats having our pill bottles scattered around. Lord knows we have enough to start a small pharmacy! And this includes our "pill graveyard." (Those meds we've stopped taking.)

 WENDY:

When I first met Honora, she made fun of my gallon-sized Ziploc bags until she realized how practical they were. It sure beat scattered bottles in a drawer! She began to do the same, and now we each have our own bags with our names Sharpied on them. We've even decorated them, doodling just for kicks. Why not try to spruce them up? When they look raggedy, we throw them out and make new ones. Who wants an old-looking pill bag?

Tip Four: Managing Your Medication

Are you feeling racy or starting to get depressed? Time to fine tune and get in to see your doctor STAT. Call for your appointment and be extra sweet to the secretary. Having a good rapport with them will get you far. The quicker you meet with your psychiatrist the better chance you have in heading off disaster.

Make sure you learn the buzz words to use with the secretary and not just say "I need to make an appointment" followed by no explanation. If you're crashing or flying high, you need them to know that. Say "I'm crashing hard, what's your first available appointment? I'll take anything!" These are desperate times. You are important! It's imperative to put yourself first; everybody else does. How can they know how dire the situation is and will continue to grow unless you make it known? Don't be afraid to prioritize and stick up for yourself. We do this when needed and they get us in! It's the squeaky wheel.

When things are fine, you're just getting refills. But if you're manic or depressed, you probably need to have your meds adjusted. Get in ASAP so your doc can adjust your meds accordingly. Here are some of the reasons why we bipolars go through needing changes to our meds.

One of the major reasons we crash is that so many of us are susceptible to Seasonal Affective Disorder or SAD. SAD is when your moods follow the seasons and you suffer horrible depression. (Some refer to it as the "winter blues.") We didn't recognize this in ourselves for quite a while. Now as we learn about ourselves, our patterns and our illness, we find we are often sensitive to seasonal changes. There are several reasons for this. One, the lack of sunlight triggers depression.

Two, throw in the letdown of the holidays, which can leave us feeling blue, and there is a bonfire of depression.

Then come spring, we have number three. On the flipside, losing that hour in March for Daylight Savings leaves us out of sync and affects our sleep. The extra daylight, even the one hour, can trigger mania. This cycle change greatly disturbs our rhythm and this can quickly become our racy season.

SOLUTIONS FOR THE BLUES:

✓ Limit your alcohol intake.

✓ Drink herbal teas vs. Caffeine (Try chamomile or peppermint).

✓ Increase exercise to boost serotonin and dopamine.

✓ Get a light box.

✓ Have your doctor adjust your doses or add meds accordingly.

SOLUTIONS FOR SPRING MANIA:

✓ Make sure you get enough sleep

✓ Don't nap during the day

✓ Avoid caffeine after mid-afternoon

✓ Have your doctor adjust your medication to prevent further mania

If you live in a year-round warm climate, not only are we jealous of you, you likely escape this group. If you do suffer from SAD, it is important to get in to see your psychiatrist, make the necessary changes to your meds and gear up for the season. For most bipolars we know, this is the standard pattern. The minute we feel racy, we are in our doctors' chairs making adjustments to our regimen. With tweaking, nipping it in the bud and a little luck, we can head off mania.

Stress might also cause you to require an adjustment to your meds. For students the added pressure of final exams can trigger mood swings. Professionals, parents and anyone with a mental illness can be affected by stress. At any given time this can throw our moods and cause a trip to our psychiatrist and/or hospital.

When you experience a lack of sleep, unmanageable stress, seasonal changes and overall depression or mania, you need to handle this with your doctor immediately. The key to adjusting your meds and avoid going down or up to the extremes is catching it early. The longer we live with this illness, the better we get at managing this.

GENERIC VS. BRAND

♦ Generic drugs are required to have the same active ingredient, strength, dosage form, and route of administration as the brand name product.

♦ Generic drugs do not need to contain the same inactive ingredients as the brand name product.

♦ The unregulated fillers vary from generic to generic.

♦ The inactive ingredients of generics are the reason why people can have different side effects on various generics.

♦ No two people and no two generics are exactly the same.

♦ 8 in 10 prescriptions filled in the US are for generic drugs.

Sources: Web.MD& US Food and Drug Administration (FDA)

 **WENDY:**

Once you have found your 'genius doctor' you have won half the battle with regard to adjusting your medication properly. They are as skilled and meticulous as a scientist. Most psychiatrists make certain to change only one med at a time and document the results. Rarely does my doctor change more than one medication at a time, as this would confuse which med is causing which change or side effect.

Every spring, when I begin to get manic, my doctor has me increase my nighttime dose of two of my meds. It's like clockwork. When hypomania of the spring/summer has subsided and fall is here, we decrease the same two meds and increase my anti-depressant. It is a regimen that has worked well. If I go outside the general wave of depression and mania, usually due to too much stress, he will make additional adjustments.

 HONORA:

It has been almost ten years since I was diagnosed with bipolar disorder. Since then, I moved from Massachusetts to New Jersey with little moves in between. I have had to switch doctors a half a dozen times. I don't feel comfortable, nor do I recommend, making medication adjustments on one's own.

When I make the call to get an appointment, which can sometimes take a week to ten days, my doctor's secretary can relay the medication adjustments he has prescribed in the interim. Oftentimes, he can look in my chart between appointments and make the decision on the spot. His secretary will call me back with his directions. It saves time, puts me on the right track, and minimizes my symptoms until I can get in to see him. When I do see him, I am already up to speed and on my way. It helps because I have a head start on the increased or decreased dose. However, if my condition is critical, he makes certain to get me in ASAP.

Tip Five: Side Effects

All medications produce some type of side effects. Everyone is different, so while one person can tolerate them, another person may not, even at various doses. You may not notice any side effects for a particular med and choose to stay on it. That is great! We wish that for you. But if you do, it is important to discuss them with your doctor and weigh the risks vs. benefits. Most of us live with the ones we can tolerate and switch what we cannot. It's a bit like dating: you try it out and when you notice the negatives, decide if you can live with them. If not, switch and try another one.

Researching side effects on reliable websites like www. *WebMD.com* or *www.Drugs.com* is useful in matching them with the medications you are taking. To help, we've prepared a list for you. It includes the most common side effects, but it's not a complete list. For a complete list, read the pamphlets the pharmacy gives you when you pick up your prescription and consult with your doctor. Always report side effects to your doctor and decide with him/her if it is a manageable option for you.

 HONORA:

I am very sensitive to medications. Period. And with every one, I experience some sort of side effect within the first ten days. It's like clockwork. (Although it usually takes me four to six weeks to know if it is working.) Many times, my body acclimates to the medication. I level off and things run smoothly. But there are medications I cannot tolerate.

For years, Wendy and I took the same medication (Topamax). Cognitively, we both got the "fuzzy brain" effect at higher doses, where we couldn't retrieve a word as fast as we wanted. That didn't stop us from taking it as it really helped us. Physically, though, while she only experienced periodic, slight aches, I had severe side pain. Even at a lower dose, it was simply too painful.

A staple in my medication arsenal for five years has been lithium. It is responsible for getting and keeping me stable. After prolonged lithium use, it caused me goiters and hypothyroidism, which is not life-threatening and can be treated. I continue taking lithium today while my endocrinologist monitors the nodules on my thyroid and my lithium levels. I have not had to have treatment for my thyroid and there has been no growth of the benign nodules in over two years. Lithium is one of the most effective medications for bipolar disorder, and it has been in use for over fifty years. I continue to stay on it and am grateful for its effectiveness.

I never would have been so informed regarding medications had it not been for the Internet. I Google the meds I take and the amount of information that pops up is astounding. It pays to research, listen to your body and talk to your doctor about your side effects. Had it not been for all three, I wouldn't have solved the Topamax and side pain mystery.

COMMON BIPOLAR DISORDER MEDICATIONS AND THEIR SIDE EFFECTS

Depakote: Dizziness, drowsiness, double vision, diarrhea, change in menstrual cycles, tremors, weight changes.

Effexor: Changes in vision, headache, high blood pressure, chest pain, ringing in ears.

Lamictal: Blurred vision, unsteadiness, double vision and in rare cases, a serious rash.

Latuda: Drowsiness, shaking, muscle stiffness, weight gain, inability to keep still and agitation.

Lithium Carbonate: Poor memory, irregular heartbeat, frequent urination, increased thirst, hand tremors, weight gain. Potential thyroid and/or liver complications.

Prozac: Restlessness, hives or itching, joint or muscle pain.

Risperdal: Agitation, decreased sexual desire, loss of balance, hand tremors, memory problems, skin rash.

Seroquel: Chills, cold sweats, lightheadedness when standing up, drowsiness, weight gain.

Topamax: Vision problems, tingling sensation, clumsiness, trouble paying attention, speech problems.

Viibryd: Nausea, diarrhea, dizziness, trouble sleeping, changes in sexual ability.

Wellbutrin: Anxiety, dry mouth, irregular heartbeat, restlessness, shaking, trouble sleeping.

Zoloft: Decreased sexual ability, aggressiveness, diarrhea, dryness of the mouth, irregular heartbeat.

Source: Web MD

Tip Six: Choosing Your Pharmacy

Pharmacies are crucial to us bipolars, so it's important to take into account all the factors and pick the best one for you. There are chains like *CVS* and *Rite Aid*, local family pharmacies and wholesale pharmacies such *Costco* and *BJ's*. You can even fill your prescriptions while shopping at the grocery store. The popular *Walmarts* also have a pharmacy.

Each pharmacy has its advantages and disadvantages concerning them all. Like finding the right meds, it helps to think of it as dating; be choosy and shop around. Remember: you are not locked in. With one swift phone call you can switch.

 WENDY:

Honora and I go to different pharmacies and have always disagreed on this one. I prefer my local family pharmacy. I started going there when I worked around the corner and they were open until 10pm, so at the time it was as convenient as could be. They always filled my scripts and had me out of there in five to ten minutes. I also liked their generics better. Plus, as silly as this sounds, they have great cards and not much to buy, so I couldn't get in trouble shopping. They closed recently, so I'm bummed and back to a chain.

The only plus is the chain is two minutes from where we live and they have a drive-through. I love the drive through! I can jump in the car and look hideous with my hair sticking out every which way. It's fantastic! It does feel impersonal and corporate, but there are two nice clerks and I focus on the positive side: the convenience is impossible to beat, prices are competitive and they have a drive-through!

My advice is to choose your pharmacy based on a combination of factors, including price, and what works best for you at the time. Don't be afraid to switch; one phone call is all it takes.

I have made what I call mini-switches depending on situations. For example, ten years ago, while going to a chain pharmacy, I wasn't responding well to several Lamictal generics. (You can find the drug manufacturer on the bottom corner of the bottle label.) Therefore, I had to hunt around for other generics to try. Chains get whatever generic comes off the truck that day, so it differs. I find better quality of generics at family pharmacies, so I began calling there first. I can't tolerate all the generics of Lamictal I've tried. So I require the brand. I've had to, on occasion, pay out of pocket when my insurance denied it. Lamictal costs a fortune without insurance, so I went to Costco because they had the cheapest. At times, I have had to change pharmacies for one med in a pinch like this.

> *HOT TIP*
> **www.goodrx.com**
> gives you the cost of generics at
> pharmacies in your area.
> Just enter your medication and zip code.
> *Voila!*

HONORA:

Unlike Wendy, I like the chain pharmacies. I go to CVS nearby and have gone there for many years. I have a good rapport with the Pharmacist-in-Charge, and he looks out for me. When I had a new med with possible complications with another med I was on, he took me aside to tell me. The relationship I have with my pharmacist is very important to me. I have tried Wendy's pharmacies as we have moved, but I always come back to my faithful, local CVS. I'm not a huge fan of their auto-refill as I'm a bit of a control freak, but I do like their automated text system; once they have filled my script, they shoot me a text to let me know it is done.

Believe it or not, this decision is more important than you may think, especially if you have to take generics and are sensitive. I am not as sensitive to generics as Wendy, but many are, so it's wise to look at the label and find out how you react and which manufacturer your pharmacy is dispensing. Also, if you don't have insurance and you need to pay out of pocket, this could weigh in at which pharmacy you choose. Not all pharmacies charge the same price for medications. Call around.

WHAT TO CONSIDER BEFORE PICKING YOUR PHARMACY:

♦ Are their hours convenient for you?
♦ Are you getting the best prices? (See our hot tip!)
♦ Do you trust the pharmacist?
♦ Are they close to home?

Tip Seven: Medication Assistance

There are several ways to get medication assistance. You can try one of the non-profits listed below. Or, you can go directly to the manufacturer's website and apply through their patient assistance program. When you go to the manufacturers' websites, look for the "assistance" or "prescription savings program" tab and follow the instructions. They will want a lot of information from you, so be prepared to gather some financial documents, but don't let it deter you. The income requirements are low and strict. If you are lucky and deemed qualified, they will give you a pre-determined number of months' worth of medication. It is typically a three- to six-month supply; each company has a set amount, so you will still need to work on a long-term plan in the meantime.

These resources could be a great route and time saver if you need medication assistance. It will take time, though. Fax whenever possible versus mailing. Ask your doctor for samples to keep you going if he/she has them.

Don't forget to price the generic of the brand and try those before deeming the brand is what you need. It could save you a lot of hassle and we all respond to each generic differently. Keep going until you get what you need and good luck!

 WENDY:

One time, I needed Lamictal, but my insurance denied coverage for the brand. I cannot tolerate the generics and tank on them. I fought for it and had to appeal my insurance company. (And finally won! So fight if you need it!) In the meantime, I went to the manufacturer of Lamictal's site to apply for their PAP (Patient Assistance Program) and was rejected. The income requirements, as most are, are very low. I was a smidge above their limit so I didn't qualify. Still, it's worth a try if you need a brand and don't respond to the generics. It is a battle, so don't forget to exhaust your generic options. Use *www.goodrx.com* to check around for the best price.

- -

BEST NON-PROFIT SITES FOR PRESCRIPTION HELP:

- Needy Meds www.needymeds.org (978) 865-4115
- Partnership for Prescription Assistance www.pparx.org
  (888) 477-2669
- RxAssist www.rsassist.org
- RxHope www.rxhope.com (877) 267-0517

- -

Chapter 2

NIGHTY NIGHT

Tip Eight: Love thy Sleep

Like a snake in the grass, mania is always lying in wait. It loves to attack when we aren't getting enough sleep. Even having poor, restless sleep one night can make us get racy the next day. Stay up a night or two and it can throw us into full-fledged mania. Why do we need sleep? Easy: sleep is the other half of our medication.

Discuss your sleep patterns with your psychiatrist. Any mood swings you may be having could be directly related to how well or not well you sleep. Instead of a med change you may just need to adjust your sleep habits. Why not keep a sleep diary and bring it in to your next appointment? Not thrilled with the idea? At least talk about it. We do. It is, after all, the other half of our medication and damn well important.

 WENDY:

In college, when people asked when I slept, my motto was "I'll get enough sleep when I'm dead." I thought I was having the time of my life when other people were asleep. And that they were missing out. How very manic of me. It's no wonder I was diagnosed soon after. Shocker.

In my early twenties, while working in New York City, once again, sleep took a back seat. At my next job I was up all night programming computers, and my wheels continued to spin non-stop. It wasn't until my late twenties when I had a 9-5 job that I practiced at sleep stability. It was the pattern and commitment to wellness I lacked before.

WAYS TO IMPROVE YOUR SLEEP

◆ **Set a specific time to go to bed**

Go to bed at or close to the same time every night. Though it's tempting to stay up later on the weekends, it can disrupt your sleep schedule. Try setting a timer if you need help remembering when to pack it in.

◆ **Wake up at the same time every morning**

If you are getting enough shut-eye, you should be able to wake up naturally, even without an alarm. With the meds we take, this may not be your reality. In this case, set as many alarms as necessary to wake up!

◆ **Nap only to "catch up"**

If you didn't sleep well the night before, a nap can help regulate you. Try to limit your nap to no more than a half hour or this can backfire and wreck your cycle.

◆ **Use black-out shades**

Try black-out shades to keep you from waking with the early morning sun.

◆ **Exercise**

Exercising tires you out and causes more restful sleep.

◆ **Light**

Increase your daytime light exposure.

 HONORA:

I never realized how important sleep was for my illness. As a new mom I always took naps with my children. But overall, I was sleep deprived. Most moms can relate to being up at 5 a.m.

and not going to bed until 11 p.m. or midnight. I didn't know it then, but my severe moods swings directly related to my sleep pattern.

Today, gratefully, I get eight to ten hours of sleep every night unless I'm off or our upstairs neighbor wakes me up prematurely. And it happens, unfortunately. When I'm depressed or manic, I tend to sleep more because I either don't want to get out of bed or I have to take extra sleep medication (Seroquel) to knock me out so I can sleep.

Tip Nine: Wind it Down

Winding down is a gradual process. We've found that nighttime is often hard for us to come down and fall asleep. So we've learned to do it progressively. Some tips we've gathered have helped us ease into bed for a restful sleep.

Our doctor recommended a long time ago that we don't watch television in our bedroom. He has said the bedroom is for sleeping, no electronics allowed. When he first said this, years ago, I thought "no, not the TV!" Now it is not a big deal and we are used to it. Although this may sound obvious, it is a good way of thinking of it as just that. Electronics distract us at night and make it difficult for us to wind down. We leave watching TV in the living room. Once in a blue moon we'll watch a show in bed, but for us, it's a bad habit.

We found we were having a hard falling asleep and timing our meds. When is the best time to take them? Staggering them before bedtime was suggested, but we still couldn't get the timing right. Now we take half of our sleep medication an hour (Wendy) to two hours (Honora) before bed and the rest as we are about to get in bed. In between, we have plenty of time to do our nightly rituals, such as washing our faces and brushing our teeth.

DID YOU KNOW? LACK OF SLEEP CAN RESULT IN:

♦ Feeling depressed or worried

♦ Increased moodiness/anxiety

♦ Difficulty concentrating

♦ Mania and/or manic episodes

♦ Increased risk of accidental death

 WENDY:

When I lived alone, it was easier for me to wind down. I had a nighttime routine with no disturbances. For example, I would fall asleep to one of those peaceful music stations on TV and set the timer for a half hour. It timed perfectly as it would turn off when I was already asleep. It was quiet and there was no noise other than the music. There were no roommates, noisy neighbors or even pets in my bed. I was in a long-time rhythm sleep-wise which also helped.

Today, I use reading. Once I am in bed and reading, I begin to drift off. I've found it to be the most effective way for me to fall asleep. It stands to reason the more wound up I am, the more winding down I need. And it is a process, no doubt, but I have gotten better at it over the years. It takes practice and dedication, but I need to tell my brain I am in control by setting a peaceful stage.

WINDING DOWN TIPS:

✓ After dinner, turn off a few lights around house.

✓ Put on comfy clothes or pajamas early.

✓ Don't go in to your bedroom until you're ready to sleep.

✓ NO TV in the bedroom.

✓ Read yourself to sleep.

✓ Set a time to go in to your bedroom and stick to it.

✓ Use alarms at night to signal when to take p.m. meds and bedtime meds. This directs you to where you should be.

✓ Scale back your schedule earlier and gradually if you are out of sync.

✓ If you are still having trouble, get in to see your doc for possible med adjustment.

Tip Ten: The Sweet Sound of Sleep

We had never heard of the white noise machine before. It was suggested to us as a way to block out noise by Wendy's psychologist. She talked about it as if everyone knew what these were. The first time we used one we fell in love with it. You will see them on the floor outside psychologists' and/or therapists' offices. They muffle the sounds of private conversations. White noise machines cost about fifty dollars at Amazon.com. They look archaic, but are the best noise machines we've ever tried.

If you cannot buy one, you can also use a fan or air conditioner works well in the warmer months. We also use an air purifier that makes a good amount of noise. In the summer it is like a trifecta of humming in our bedroom: the white noise machine, the air conditioner and the air purifier! If you don't have any of the above, try a fan. Doesn't everyone have a fan?

WENDY:

Had Dr. Kamm not given me her white noise machine, I might never have learned about my favorite sleep wellness item. There are also other sound machines I've tried, ones with a variation of soothing sounds: brooks, wind, crickets and other assortments. (Beware of the ones that make water noises . . . it may . . . um . . . not go so well. No further comment.)

HONORA:

Your smartphone has an app for noise machines, too. There is even one called White Noise Machine. We discovered it and now use it for travel versus lugging around our machine. Once we forgot to pack our beloved white noise machine and scrambled for a solution. There it was: the white noise app solution! On a Droid, go to the "Play Store" widget; on the iPhone it's the "App Store." There are many free apps you can download right onto your phone. If your cell phone is plugged in overnight, you don't even have to worry about draining your battery.

Tip Eleven: Blackout Shades

We were having a tough time sleeping in the morning with the light coming into our bedroom. A lot of light came in despite closing the shades and placing the bed so as to avoid it. We closed our blinds tightly, but it didn't matter; the light managed to infiltrate.

One day at Aunt Carol's house, we were complaining that we were waking up too early because of the bright sun.

"Blackout shades!" Aunt Carol exclaimed.

"What?" We had heard of them, but didn't know much else.

"They are great! I used them when I was nursing." Aunt Carol was an ICU nurse who used to work long, overnight shifts; she needed them to block out the daytime light. She slept during the day.

As fast as you can say "nighty night," off we went to Lowe's and picked out a pair with thick brown fabric. It doesn't let much light in and we sleep like babies. Thank God for blackout shades! Whoever invited them is a genius.

It should be noted, though, that at first we missed the morning light and slept in, often past when we wanted to get up. (We can sleep through several alarms thanks to Seroquel!) You can use what they call a "dawn stimulator." It mimics the sun. You can set timers, alarms, they can come on gradually. There is a whole world of help you can use in conjunction with your blackout shades. Mix it up! We love 'em all!

Chapter 3

DRUGS, ALCOHOL AND THE "INES"

Tip Twelve: Illegal Drugs are a No-No

Not doing drugs is a wise choice for anyone, mentally ill or not. This is obvious. For those with bipolar disorder, illegal drug use can launch you into a full blown, drug-induced manic episode. It can cause more frequent and severe mood swings and lessen the effectiveness of medications. It also increases the risk of suicide.

So here's the deal, plain and simple: drugs wreck your life, land you in jail, can take your life and in the least, ensure that your medication has little to zero chance of working. If you are doing them, please get help. If you don't believe any of the above, you are fooling yourself. This is the truth and we know firsthand.

 WENDY:

Unfortunately, I had to learn this one the hard way. I was diagnosed while in a drug-induced episode in college. Pot was my drug of choice, and I swore I would never do anything harder than that. I was a carefree hippy girl, a deadhead, and I was terrified of acid or anything stronger. When I turned twenty-six though, all bets were off. There he was, my co-worker-turned-boyfriend and eventual partner in crime. Joe (not his real name) introduced me to cocaine and that's when my life went down the tubes fast.

During one short year, I had become reduced to someone I didn't want to know, let alone be. I'm lucky I got help when I did and have stayed away from it since then. Unfortunately, there are some who don't survive and it is common. Overdose and bipolar often go hand in hand though I wish to God they didn't. I had a close friend who overdosed on a mix of cocaine and heroin and she died while I was writing my first book. No one knew what she was doing until after she died. She is missed by many, many friends and family.

> It is reported that 60-70% of bipolars are addicted to alcohol and/or drugs. In order for proper diagnosis and our meds to work, addiction needs to be treated.

 HONORA:

I was never a consistent drug user, but I always took what was offered to me. I wasn't one to turn down a "good time." Eventually though, a marijuana charge got me into trouble with the law. Mania and illegal substances go hand in hand.

I wasn't able to connect the dots. Manic episodes + drugs/ alcohol = arrests. It wasn't until I was a few years sober and on the right combination of meds that I was able to see the pattern. It's clear as day to me today. And thankfully, because the drugs and alcohol have been removed from the equation, half the battle has been won. The other half of the battle is keeping my meds on track.

Tip Thirteen: Limit or Eliminate Alcohol

Most psychiatric medications warn us to not mix alcohol with them. Not only do they react negatively with one another, but it can stop your meds from working altogether. It is a sticker on nearly every bottle we have. It's the one with the droopy eye. We love that one. "May cause drowsiness." We're already drowsy!

Why do we reach for alcohol? Some of us are alcoholics, true. For the rest, the theory is that alcohol is a way for bipolars to self-medicate. We love to do that! For people with bipolar disorder, we are five times more likely to misuse alcohol than the rest of the population. This staggering number is understandable given our unstable moods. Alcohol is a depressant, though we often grab for it during low moods.

Your doctor can advise you better, but we were told not to drink on our medications. Some might say a drink is okay, but every psychiatrist we've ever been to has advised us against it.

 WENDY:

My very first psychiatrist told me I couldn't drink, and I flipped out. I could not imagine all the events where I would not be able to drink at and I became resentful. I didn't care that it was for the medication's sake. All I cared about was the perceived dent in my not-so-raging-anyway social life that it would create. Really, it was because I was an active alcoholic and didn't want to face the music at the time.

The second psychiatrist did, too. In my late twenties, I gave up alcohol altogether. One drink to me is never enough. I cannot stop. It has been ten years since I have had a drink and no one misses that girl, most of all me. Still, even if I could, I doubt I would because it's not worth it in my opinion. That's like getting foot surgery and walking on it the day after, despite doctor's orders. It defeats the purpose.

I say watch the booze and give your meds, your illness and yourself a chance.

> According to the National Institute of Mental Health, people with bipolar disorder are 5 times more likely to develop alcohol misuse and dependence than the rest of the population.

 HONORA:

I drank alcohol for years. A lot of alcohol. It started in high school, moved on to college, and then continued through my adult life. As the years went on, my consumption increased dramatically. Two or three beers became five or six—each night—weekends, all bets were off. Since I never missed a day of work, I didn't think I had a problem.

I became so miserable that I decided, reluctantly, to see a psychiatrist. I was terrified at the idea, but more terrified at the idea of having to live the way I was living. My doctor, Dr. Merrill (not his real name), saw right through me. As we began the preliminary session, he zeroed right in on my drinking habits. As I was giving him the rundown on my behaviors in the last few years, he was quick to point out that I had an alcohol problem. He also thought I could very well have bipolar disorder, but he was leery to diagnose me bipolar until I got sober; the behaviors can be similar and misleading.

I took the meds Dr. Merrill gave me, but I couldn't get sober. It was a struggle for a time; like a see-saw. When I got a period of sobriety, he was able to confidently diagnose me as having bipolar disorder. I didn't feel wonderful right away, but it was such a relief to finally know what was "wrong" with me.

Tip Fourteen: Twelve-Step Groups

This tip saves lives. Many people who have bipolar disorder suffer from a number of addictions. When the mentally ill are alcoholics or drug addicts, the term used is M.I.C.A., which stands for Mentally Ill Chemically Addicted. The nickname for those of us that fall in to the category is: "Double Trouble." It can be a rough ride, but there is help, a lot of help, and the twelve-step groups are lifesavers. They're free, which is the cheapest help you will ever receive. When you treat the addiction, be it alcohol, drugs or what have you, you can then properly treat your bipolar disorder. Otherwise, your meds don't have a snowball's chance in hell.

To help with addiction, there are a number of twelve step meetings you can attend for support. There is A.A. (Alcoholics Anonymous), which is the founding father of them all. From this group, many other life-saving twelve-step meetings have been born. A.A. is a wonderful organization that is worldwide. There is N.A. (Narcotics Anonymous), Al-Anon, (which supports loved ones of alcoholics and addicts) and many others. Al-Anon has changed countless families for the better. There are a number of anonymous programs for bipolars, and their families can partake and get better in.

Alcoholics Anonymous
(800) 245-1377
www.aa.org

•

Narcotics Anonymous
(818) 773-9999
www.na.org

•

Al-Anon
(888) 425-2666
www.al-anon.alateen.org

You name it, and there's a twelve-step group for it. Do yourself a favor—if you need help with an addiction—check them out. Even if you don't have an addiction, perhaps your spouse, partner or other supportive loved one does. Al-Anon can be a tremendous support network for you. No matter what your circumstance, you'll gain a trusted support person in your sponsor and an instant second family. What's to lose?

Twelve-step programs save lives. Addictions are progressive and fatal; most alcoholics and addicts cannot stop on their own. The strength and hope in twelve-step groups provide bipolars (and anyone) with the support system they need to quit. Al-Anon has also helped millions get the support they need and is a fantastic organization. They provide tremendous help for loved ones of the alcoholics and addicts.

You can easily go on the internet, type in A.A., N.A. or Al-Anon into any search engine and find your way to meetings. Or, go directly to their websites we have listed. There are literally thousands of meetings across the United States. If you feel uncomfortable going you might try bringing a friend for moral support to an "Open Meeting" (usually listed as "OS").

Remember it is anonymous, so what you say and whom you see there, will stay there. If you feel nervous about going in your area, you can always go to a meeting fifteen or twenty minutes away. Get some help, try it out and bring a loved one for support to need a push to get started.

Tip Fifteen: The Caffeine Blackout

Caffeine is a stimulant and can be ammunition for hypomania and mania. When one of us is displaying hypomania, or feeling a tad racy even, the other turns into the "caffeine police." Immediately, we turn our coffee station—we use the Keurig cups—to decaf to be supportive of one another. Thus the caffeine blackout is in place.

Becoming the "caffeine police" is not much fun, true, but it's better than your loved one becoming even more manic. If you live alone it requires more discipline, but it can be done. Remember, it's your health we're talking about.

Among individuals who experience periodic
panic attacks, scientists have learned
that they can trigger an attack
by giving large amounts of caffeine.

•

Even in someone without a mood disorder,
too much caffeine can cause nervousness,
agitation, rapid or irregular heartbeat,
dizziness, and mood changes.

Tip Sixteen: Nicotine the Other "Ine"

Nicotine is a stimulant. Besides the many health risks it poses, it is not good for our mania.

Although it seems like a no-brainer to quit, and it is, it's very hard to do. It often requires several tries and above all: a conscious commitment to our health. You'll save a ton of money, eliminate that awful smell, make your loved ones happy, and feel healthier. Plus, eliminating another stimulant goes in your favor while trying to control mania. Some try patches, some gum, some wean using e-cigarettes to quitting as a psychological step—though they contain nicotine, too. Some try Chantix and some opt for a combination of methods. Others quit cold turkey. Often people utilize support groups, national quit dates and online or phone assistance. Whatever it takes, it is worth it. A reward system helps, too. Give it all a try and find what works for you. Remember, if at first you don't succeed, try, try again!

 WENDY:

We are certainly sympathetic and painfully aware of the process and struggles of quitting smoking. Nicotine, as the doctor in the hospital pointed out while I sat there clutching my patch, is harder to quit than heroin. "Fantastic!" I said. There's nothing like trying to overcome depression and being without your nicotine at the same time! Let alone trying to quit at all!

It has always been a telltale sign to me of how manic I was getting by the number of cigarettes that were in my ashtray.

I began smoking in my twenties and smoked for a decade. I was ashamed to be the only smoker in my family. Then I quit and was smoke-free for three years. I started smoking again for a couple years and am happy to report I'm smoke-free for over a year now. It's a healthy choice but not easy.

 ## HONORA:

It is not easy to quit smoking. I have been trying for years. I have done it all—the patch, gum, even Chantix. I would be successful for a few months, but always go back to smoking. It's frustrating that I can't break this habit. I have just recently tried something new—the e-cigarette. It is an electronic ciga-rette that has a small amount of nicotine, but not all the harmful smoke and carcinogens of regular cigarettes. I feel like I am going in the right direction and hope to be successful this time around. This, by far, has been the most difficult addiction for me to combat. It is a primary goal, and I am determined to get this monkey off my back.

> "There are 45 million cigarette compared to 2.5 million e-cigarette smokers in the U.S." —*Time*, January 2013

Chapter 4

SEX, MONEY AND ROCK & ROLL

Tip Seventeen: Watch the Manic Sex

Mania and sex go together like hot fudge and sundaes. Unfortunately, there is a big difference between calories and risky sexual behavior. We're not talking about sex with your spouse or partner. We're talking *manic* sex. The kind that doesn't care who you are having it with. If we rounded up a bunch of bipolars, and sat around a campfire, lord *knows* the stories we would hear! It would certainly be an entertaining evening, wouldn't it?

To get serious though, manic bipolars often find themselves on chat websites that lead to dangerous meetings with strangers. Meeting a stranger is not safe. In the least, you could catch an STD; worse, you could get pregnant or get killed. It is playing on the tracks, though. At the time who is thinking of consequences?

There could be permanent repercussions. We are left to pick up the pieces and take responsibility afterwards, though it is impossible to see the damage unfolding. Our prefrontal lobe is shot while we're looking at the guy or gal next to us and thinking they are the cat's meow. No manic bipolar can process what they're doing or see consequences logically. There is a medical reason. There is not enough prefrontal lobe present.

We often get down on ourselves and don't realize this. That is like asking a child what their bedtime is and saying "okay, you can go to bed at midnight." When you are making the rules while manic, *of course* sex with strangers makes sense. The more sex the better! Who cares about consequences? We are not thinking about the clean up after the party. It is only the party that counts.

That is also like teenage behavior. "Hey everyone: party at my house. My parents are away!" The problem is, your parents do return. Your hypothalamus does return to full functioning and there is a mess to clean up and explain. It's almost difficult to do. "I was drunk. I don't understand how this place got so messy." "I only intended to have a few friends over." To us, this is the same principle. We have had some parties and explaining to do. They start off small, but what a mess they can become! It is the same principle as manic sex: our limited mentality just tells us to clean up the party after the party is over. The trouble is always the inevitable relationship cleanup. In the most severe case: you could get raped or murdered. It all happens and mania is often the culprit at the helm.

You could lose the trust of the one you love and ruin your relationship or marriage beyond repair. Haven't you seen those shows on TV about being unfaithful? Applied to a sexual spree, you must multiply it. With a bipolars' risky sexual behavior, it depends on your loved one if they'll take you back. Part of it is understanding the illness and what is happening in our brains causing this behavior. Part is being honest and accepting responsibility, even if our brain may be malfunctioning. What happens is a decision reached by both parties. Mania is fascinating on a scientific level; however, it can be tragic on a personal one.

If you realize what you're doing while you're doing it, our advice is to seek immediate medical attention to control your mania. Also, get honest and be sure to explain to your psychologist/therapist/doctor what is going on. Unfortunately, we don't often out ourselves during an episode, especially a major one; however, your loved ones may catch on. The good news here is your professionals can intervene and counsel you both. We suggest you get honest with the people who can help you medically and bring your loved one to counseling with you. You'll probably need help.

 WENDY:

When I was manic and hypersexual, I chose to have sex with people I wouldn't have otherwise looked twice at. You should've seen the guy I met during my first manic episode in college! He was twice my age with a huge beer belly. In my twenties and thirties I made some horrible choices. They would've fit in to a police line-up quite well, actually. What saved me is eventually disclosing it to my psychologist and close friend. This didn't happen right away; I was manic, after all. It was intoxicating and the more manic I got, the worse I became. Finally, the gig was up because I knew what I was doing was wrong. First, I confided in a friend. I needed to hear from someone else what I already knew. I chose someone who was loving and gentile with me, and it was a relief to let my secret out.

Next, I told my psychologist whom I see more regularly than my psychiatrist. I have more time with her, so I can fill in the blanks. I was single when displaying this behavior. I'm one of the lucky ones; the worst thing that happened to me was sand in my bed and ultimately, the guilt after the mania. The guilt was the worst, though. I felt horrible about myself!

Tip Eighteen: Stay Off the Sex Sites

If you are manic and hypersexual there is a chance you could frequent sex sites. This could mean: the "dating" sex sites. These are the ones with the steamy commercials. You know, the ones that egg you on with late night ads to cater to your loneliness. We don't need any added incentive to try to quench our hyper-sexuality when manic. They had us at toll-free. All it takes is a little nudge and our bad decisions come floating in like the bad perfume smell of a passerby. We're hooked.

Unfortunately, many of us have learned the hard way. If we're lucky, we have learned our lesson and retreated unscathed. If not, there is collateral damage. With any luck, you will heed our warnings and spare yourself the trouble here. There is nothing fun about sex sites. Usually the people on there are the bottom of the barrel. Remember, these are not good decision making times; consequently, these are also not people we would ordinarily have coffee with. Let alone meet.

The internet sex sites are a prime location for finding these individuals. There are very few decent people on there looking for companionship. The majority are looking for a quick fix, like a diabetic looking for a quick sugar boost when woozy. And if they are looking and receiving, they have a high potential to screw you over while giving you a disease. Stay clear; the chat rooms may excite you, but if you meet them, they're often damaged goods. Aren't we, after all, when we're manic? Think about it: why would they need to go online to get their tail? They must be desperate, or married, or up to no good in general. Just like us when we're manic.

Do yourself a favor and don't bother. Get in to see your doc to adjust meds and in the meantime, figure out a way to be safe. If you're manic, and married, your partner could be lucky! Anything is better than meeting someone and risking your health, relationship and life. Be careful, be safe and get help fast.

WENDY:

I am lucky here, in a sense. There was only one time when I did the internet sex craze. It was in 2006 during my last major manic episode. It started out innocently enough, as they often do. I was lonely and watching TV one night. There it was a commercial for a website that practically called my name. I signed up on the dating site and received one response in the first week. My profile was not racy. As I progressed and got more manic, my curiosity at the "intimate encounters" side peaked. I clicked on it and added it to my profile. Next thing I knew, I had tons of guys vying for my attention. I couldn't keep up with all of the conversations!

Previously, I was like a disease on dating websites and here I was a steak to the lions. It was fun, naughty and playing on the edge. Would I meet them? Could I? I chose a select few and did. Often it was for coffee or dinner first. Some didn't get past coffee. Case in point: there was the weirdo that ordered chicken soup, wouldn't take off his coat, then asked for a picture of me. He was creepy as hell. Like I said, some didn't get past "check please." I shouldn't have had sex with any of them, but when mania is calling, you tend to pack a suitcase and run.

HONORA:

I began chatting with people in chat rooms and then once I got to "know" them, we'd do video chats. I was fascinated by it all. It got racy real fast. There were many people to choose from, too! (I was manic back then and not medicated.) It wasn't unusual for me to fly to Chicago, Wisconsin, or Vegas for the weekend just to meet these people. What was I thinking?

Tip Nineteen: Music for Mood

If you are down, try putting on a song you know will cheer you up. Feeling manic? How about some calm music to slow your mind down? Of course, when we're manic last thing we want to do is put on calm music.

Sometimes, we have to change the station or CD for each other to help the other person. For example, when Honora or I realize that the other one is racy, we'll select a calmer CD or station and vice-versa. When we're manic, we want to blast music from our car or at home. The louder the better. The more frenetic, sign us up!

What would truly help, is to put on the type of music that's opposite our mood. Try this and see how it works. At first it will feel odd, but your mind will thank you. Try it when you're down, or having a bad day. It's no cure for depression; you can't fool your brain out of depression. You can, though, demand a few minutes or hours of musical happiness if you program the right tunes.

 **WENDY:**

I used to play classical piano as a child and it soothed me, but these days it's the *last* thing I think of to put on when I'm manic. Recently though, I noticed I was feeling racy and did exactly what we're suggesting you do: I put on calm music. It was a classical station programmed on my dad's car. (I borrowed it for the day; my car was in the shop.) My brain felt more comfortable; it is the only way I can describe it. I felt calmer as I drove around all day. It was odd at first, and I felt confused and uncomfortable for a few minutes. I stuck with it, though, refrained from changing the station, and in no time, it was soothing. It was as if I was giving my brain a rest and it appreciated it!

Tip Twenty: Money Troubles

While we are manic, money is no object. Our stories range from buying luxury cars to losing it all in Vegas to shopping sprees; we have heard it all and everything in between. The problem is the manic bipolar has no awareness of the bottom line. Balances in accounts? Who knows what those are. Limits? No such thing. Debit cards? Disaster! The last thing we want is for you or anyone to pull the plug on fun and relinquish control. It feels like defeat, as if we've lost the scoring goal in overtime.

Cleanup after a manic episode of spending is nasty. If you're lucky, your bank statement will say zero. Often, it will be negative. After you stabilize, though, you'll regret it all!

What has helped us is to develop a game plan so history doesn't keep repeating itself. Money does matter and you will need it later. The time to plan is when we're stable. The time to enact is as soon as manic behavior is detected by either person; usually by our loved ones.

If there is a particular time of the year when you overspend due to mania, and you know this is your pattern, anticipate and plan. This financial, proactive action is a white flag, a surrender, which is a bit of a pride buster; however, if you do this, you'll be happy you saved yourself money after the manic episode has come and gone.

{ Have a problem with your credit cards?
Do what Suze Orman suggests:
Put your cards in a jar and
freeze them! }

 **WENDY:**

Although I have been through a few manic episodes, and have overspent money in all of them, I am just learning how to cope and relinquish control. I was never in a relationship before, so the consequences of blowing all of my money fell on me. Now I am in a partnership and learning about collateral damage and behavior modification. With two bipolars in the house, after years of fumbling, we had to establish some rules. I am far worse than Honora in the money department.

Notably, I have learned to relinquish my bank cards to Honora when I am manic. The idea doesn't come from me, ever; she notices my mania first and points it out. I clutch on to them hard as I turn them over! This has proven to be a great solution, although it sucks at the time. We also move to the cash system. I am given a specific, small amount of cash. There is a reserve in the car for gas and I keep one check on me for emergencies. When I go to the grocery store or to a doctor's appointment, I get the debit card for that trip only.

There is always a solution. It helped that my psychologist worked with us to find one that worked for both of us. She also had input on when she felt I wasn't manic anymore and could responsibly spend again. That took the pressure off Honora being the bad guy, which helped take the financial/ mania strain off our relationship.

HONORA:

It is inconceivable to me, but I blew through fifteen thousand dollars during a manic episode in 2008. The episode couldn't have lasted more than two months. Of course my parents were concerned and spoke to me about it, but I said I had it under control. I had always been a responsible spender.

In quick succession, I bought a computer, a cell phone, a GPS for my car and applied for credit cards, all of which I had already owned. At the end of my spree I could not even pay my rent! My parents had to bail me out—again. This disaster could have been avoided had I given up control of my finances. It was a painful lesson.

Chapter 5

DOCTORS, PSYCHOLOGISTS AND YOUR SUPPORT TEAM

Tip Twenty-One: Finding the 'One'

Get the best doctor you can. Period. We cannot emphasize how important this is. If you don't have a doctor that is making a positive difference in your mental health, keep searching. They are out there!

Generally speaking, the best doctors are experienced psychiatrists in private offices who have been around a long time. We mean *decades* of experience. Their waiting rooms are full, it is hard to get appointments and they don't take insurance. Don't let that fool you; it is possible to afford it. If you can get over the hurdle of the initial visit—and it's a big hurdle—their med check appointments can be affordable. You may have to spend less on other things; but, this is your life we are talking about.

Research well who to switch to, since the initial consults are an arm and a leg. Where we live they currently range from $375 to $450. In urban areas, they are higher. Ask around and if you keep getting the same name, that is likely your answer. If you do decide to change, make sure you overlap care so you always have doctor supervision and meds. You don't want to be caught without either. Going without medications, even one of them, for any period of time will likely have serious consequences.

There are over 41,000 psychiatrists in the United States today.

There are options other than private psychiatrists. There are great doctors who are in clinics—often running them—who take patients. Personally, never have we been on as high a number of meds as when we went to a local, hospital-affiliated outpatient clinic. Often, that is where doctors start after receiving their licenses. The good news is you could be charged a sliding scale, making care more affordable. We have an excellent healthcare agency in Monmouth County, NJ called CPC Behavioral Health Care which provides for several services (mental, addiction, etc.) from one source. Each county has such agencies that are funded privately, and people can get treatment there. Our best advice is to see what agencies are present in your community and if you cannot afford it, see if they will treat you despite your inability to pay for service. We have a family member who is very happy there.

We recommend private psychiatry, but it's expensive. There is no way around it. Again, most do not accept insurance. They don't have to; they are busy and don't have the time to process insurance claims. They have some of the busiest secretaries you'll find. You can get a receipt and submit it to your insurance yourself, though. While you have to do the submitting, you can still get money back from your insurance company. It is a one page form. You have to get a receipt from the secretary and fill out that form. The coverage for an out-of-network doctor will depend on your insurance. Losing a little bit of money to see a doctor out-of-network is a small price to pay for having the most knowledgeable doctor you can.

Again, once you get past the exorbitant initial consult, you can relax. Most private, non-insurance-accepting psychiatrists will offer what they call "med checks." A med check is a quick, fifteen minute appointment where you get refills and check-in if you don't need special attention. The price in our area is under $85, and affordable, especially since we don't go every month. That first one is a killer though. We know of a mom who sold her gold jewelry to pay for her daughter's initial consult to a top psychiatrist.

There is nothing, in our opinion, more important than our health, and it goes back to having the most knowledgeable and experienced doctor. They can keep finding those delicate combinations of meds like solving a giant Rubix cube. The excellent psychiatrists get it. The newer ones don't have the experience.

Once again, if you don't feel you have the best, keep looking. It is the same principle as switching pharmacies. With one phone call you are on your way to changing to a new one. Prioritizing your health starts with finding the right doctor. We wish you well in finding "the one." Your care is the most important thing on this earth. Nothing is more important.

 **WENDY:**

I have been to four psychiatrists. It seems I have run the gamut in this area. Personally, I found the ones covered by my insurance were not as strong as the private psychiatrists who don't accept it. Top doctors earned their way through their experience, education, patients, research and knowledge. There's a reason why they cost more: they deserve it.

My journey started with the psychiatrist at Virginia Tech who diagnosed me. I hated her, but she came from Cornell, highly intelligent and qualified. She did look slightly evil to me, but again, any doctor would to us when we are in a full-blown manic episode getting diagnosed. Wouldn't they? Her area of interest was in videotaping manic bipolars and this drove me up the wall each time she asked. As it sat in the corner and she stared at me through squinted, accusing eyes (again, my manic perception), it took all I had not to throw the camera through her window. I find it fascinating now if I had that videotape of myself what I would've looked like. I realize now, of course, I was lucky she was there to diagnose me. Back then most colleges did not have psychiatrists on staff. Apparently there were enough of us flipping out and our college recognized the need. Thank God!

My next psychiatrist was a total nightmare. She was cold, and her office was cold, too! She would sit there in her mink coat while I froze, and she even ate in front of me. I detested her. Then she called me an alcoholic when I protested the "no drinking on your meds" rule. She was smug; then again I'm sure I was no treat. As soon as she called me an alcoholic, I split. (Years later, she turned out to be right.)

The third psychiatrist I had was a woman I saw for five years. She had me journal, examined my nails, which she said told her where I was at, and did therapy, too. She read my journals, which was kind of creepy now that I think about it. She knew everything about me; except the little I chose to conceal. The minute she said she thought of me like a daughter, it freaked me out. I thought she crossed the line and I was on the hunt for a new one.

I found my next psychiatrist through my insurance at work. (Which was good, it just had a crappy selection of shrinks!) I should've known when the second, third and now fourth doctor had no one in the waiting room that it was a giant red flag. He had the gall to constantly say I was depressed because of my weight. No kidding! He brought it up at every session, and I'm surprised I didn't jab his neck with a pen. (The only reason I didn't was I was too depressed.) There's nothing like a degrading shrink to make you more depressed than you already are. I was unimpressed with his skills and decided to change. Instead of leaving abruptly, I had to hang in there until I found my new doc. I needed him for refills but the curtain call was in our near future.

I asked around. My Mom asked around. We had two other friends, family members and I asked my bipolar friends, too. All told, by the time we combed the fields, we had an overwhelming consistent name: Dr. Bransfield. The appointment was made and two and a half months later, I had my initial consult. Ten years later, I am still there and will be until he retires. Although my doctor is expensive, he is worth every dollar. He is a medication wizard and it is money well spent on my mental health. Plus, I don't go every month and the med check, fifteen minute appointments make it affordable. I figure if I were going to a few doctors and paying their copays each month, it would equal one payment to my psychiatrist every few months. That makes me feel better about the cost since bipolars have high enough costs for everything.

 HONORA:

I, too, have been to several psychiatrists. Some in Massachusetts where I was first diagnosed and some in NJ when I moved back here. They have each had their expertise. My last doctor was an expert in addiction, highly ranked in his specialty. He helped me with my bipolar disorder and alcoholism treatment. My new psychiatrist is amazing, too. He is the best I have ever been to. He works with me, listens to me as we change and manage meds. Plus, he makes me laugh. Who knew you could have fun at the doctor's office?

Tip Twenty-Two: Searching for Your Psychologists, LCADCs and More

There are a myriad of specialties out there: addiction, family, child and mental illnesses. We suggest you make a list of questions for your prospective team before hiring them. Some prefer psychologists which are either PhD or PsyD. (In some states, they are now allowed to practice with their masters.) Others seek Licensed Certified Alcohol and Drug Counselors (LCADCs), Licensed Professional Counselors (LPCs) or Licensed Certified Social Workers (LCSWs). A lot of your decisions will be based on insurance or lack thereof and at what stage of your diagnosis you are in. This has been our experience.

At times, especially surrounding treating our alcoholism and addiction, we have found great value in counseling from our LCADCs. We received help and insight from them that paved the way for us. Each of us saw ours for three to four years and they were immensely helpful. Some of our friends only go to their LCADCs. Others opt to see psychologists. When we needed more help with bipolar disorder, we searched for psychologists who specialize in it. If you're lucky, you will find both if you need it. If you have any comorbidity (eating disorder, borderline personality disorder, etc.) it doesn't hurt to see if there is a psychologist out there who has experience with both.

Currently we are seeing psychologists who have their doctorates. Some have their masters now. Many LPCs have masters. Social workers vary in their education. What matters most is the understanding they have of our illness, their experience and how you work together. Also, different professionals may or may not be affordable. This is a huge factor in your decision. We tend to believe the higher the education, the better off you are, but there are always exceptions to the rule proving us wrong.

For example, we have been to psychologists who were out in space. We have been to CADCs who were amazing and gave us support unparalleled for what we needed at the time. You may find you have different needs at different times of your life. Some LPCs and social workers provide excellent integrative care and are tapped in to local resources which could help you financially and particularly at the early stages of your care. There are LPCs who provide CBT (Cognitive Behavioral Therapy) that some psychologists may not.

A great starting question to ask yourself is: what do I need? Then, make a list of questions to ask each person, analyze your financial options and make some calls. Start with the big questions such as coverage, cost, co-pay and go from there. Once you have established your parameters, you are ready to ask around for reputation. Then make your list and call to ask what experience they have in bipolar disorder. Do they specialize in mental illness? Do they treat addiction if you have it? Mainly, do they treat a lot of bipolar patients? This would be our number one question. They may not say they specialize, but they ought to have a high bipolar clientele. A lot of your decision will likely be based on finances and insurance.

Most insurance plans cover psychologists' visits. They do not, as of now, cover LCADCs. Some psychologists' copays may be as high as a visit to see a LCADC. If you choose the "wrong" psychologist (i.e. one with no experience), they may have little training in what you need. It could be a horrible match. The cost of a LCADC may be the same as psychologist copay. Without insurance, a LCADC is cheaper than a psychologist. It is a roll of the dice cost-wise, depending upon the individual person. Regarding care, LCADC can be helpful 60-75% of the time, addiction and bipolar go hand in hand. If this is not your case, going to a LCADC is futile. There are many factors to consider and the field of help for bipolars is vast, expensive and very important. Often, it is a trial and error process. Be sure to ask about their experience, specialty, and cost and feel free to switch until you receive the care you need. While we generally support seeking the care of a psychologist specializing in bipolar disorder if you can afford it, this may not always be the best fit for everyone. We have often gotten excellent care from LCADCs, especially when our focus was on drugs and alcohol at that time in our lives. You could luck out and have someone who is excellent in treating both.

Unfortunately, in the past, many insurance companies have managed to get away with limiting treatment because of social prejudice concerning emotional problems. Thanks to past Senator Patrick Kennedy and the late Senator Ted Kennedy, the lead sponsors of the mental health parity laws, health insurers are now required to treat mental health on par with physical health. It requires they cover care for mental illness and addiction no less than they cover physical care. Many states have also passed their own mental health parity laws. All of this helps us see our psychologist more which is excellent news. Perhaps someday this will extend to the other professionals we may see as well.

 WENDY:

I see a psychologist now, and am a big fan of them, but have worked with every type of professional in the mental health field at some point. I feel everyone has helped me in a different way, in various stages since my diagnosis. I have to say: there have been some wing-dingers though!

I've had social workers in programs and hospitals assigned to me. The outpatient program I attended at The Women's Trauma and Addiction Program at Princeton House gave me a one half-hour session with a LCSW each week. Local hospitals, at least in our area, give their patients a fifteen minute meeting, also with a LCSW. It is considered an "exit" or "planning strategy meeting" as they call it. (They need to know they're not throwing you out on the street. It's their policy, in fact. You have to be released *somewhere*; thus the meeting.) My grandmother was a social worker and I have the highest respect for them; they have a lot of heart despite often being the most overworked, underpaid and undervalued professionals in the field.

I have gone to two very helpful LCADCs for three years each. They were indispensable to me when I needed help with addiction. They treat a lot of mentally ill patients with addiction, like me, and knew quite a bit about bipolar disorder, though not necessarily all the ins and outs of my meds. Still, they understood the link between the two. I know three excellent, highly qualified LCADCs. As always, I encourage you to get a referral by asking around and ask if they have any bipolar clientele. This way, you know they are familiar with both bipolar disorder and addiction.

If you *don't* have an addiction, you have several options. Personally, I have received the most help from a psychologist. And this, by the way, is where I have met the wing-dingers. You might have to go through a few. I encourage you to try out one session and determine whether or not they are for you. Honora has had to do this several times as she chose her psychologist from her insurance page. She didn't have a referral. In this case, you are bound to meet a few you don't mix well with.

Regarding psychologists, I have met either the most amazing ones who are excellent at their job, or the most screwed up ones who couldn't lead you out of a paper bag. I know of two psychologists who specialize in bipolar disorder (one of whom I go to) who fall in to the first category. They are insightful and amaze me with their knowledge of the bipolar brain, medications and our behavior. Then there is the other category. Unfortunately, I spent years and years with someone from this one. She specialized in taking my money and being useless. In fact, she made me *more* depressed. Her office was depressing too and she would stare off in to space like she was lost. (It made me wonder if she was listening at all!) At the time, I was lost too, so we were a perfect match! Beware of the lost souls you may encounter in any specialty.

The amount of training psychologists go through for bipolar disorder is more than a psychiatrist. Can you believe it? That is what my psychologist told me one session and I nearly fell off the couch. After five years of school, years of working in clinics, a dissertation, passing a board and thirty years in practice, I don't think I could find someone more qualified—both educationally and experienced—with bipolar disorder. She knows everything about our brains, inside and out, and can explain anything I bring to her. My psychologist is also very knowledgeable about bipolar meds and can suggest I talk to my psychiatrist about XYZ med because I am displaying XYZ behaviors. She will even call him if I am bad enough; although she hasn't had to do so, gratefully, yet. She was close a few times. Just knowing she is on top of me is very comforting. I finally have a network, and my psychologist completed the circle.

My suggestion is: once you realize you aren't getting anywhere or don't "gel" with your therapist, ask around for the name of a good psychologist, make an appointment and move on. Make sure they specialize in bipolar disorder and not "family" or "child" psychology. You want to make sure they have experience with your illness; otherwise, it's like going to a hand doctor for your knee. If you cannot afford a psychologist, seek the help of a social worker or LCADC if you have an addiction. They can offer fantastic support, especially if they treat many bipolars. That is a key question to ask and my greatest tip.

Number one, ask around. If you scour your network of friends, family and the mental health community, you'll find someone who knows of a good psychologist. If not, go through your insurance and find a few in the area. Start calling and see if they treat any patients with bipolar disorder. (Personally, we're fans of referrals.)

Number two, give them a mini-interview on the phone to ask about their client base. Find out their years of experience, background and specialty. It doesn't hurt to research them online, either.

Once you get quality care, stay with them no matter what it takes. When I had a hard time paying the co-pay, I would periodically bring baked goods, pottery, my books; I practically tap danced on the table until I could pay the co-pay! I had a running balance and then would pay with a big chunk of money, such as a tax refund. Or, once I got caught up with my bills I would write a large check. I did anything to stay with my psychologist. If you're lucky, you'll get one who is willing to work with you. If you have a solid, working relationship and fall on hardship, sometimes you can make it work. Spread out your visits. Start baking! When you get money, set it aside and pay up! Hold on to them like they're the best relationship you've ever had.

HONORA:

Finding the right psychologist takes some work. If you have insurance you can start by going to your insurance's website. A number of participating psychologists will be listed in alphabetical order and by distance from your location. By being on this list you are assured they accept your insurance. Also, www.zocdoc.com is a user-friendly website that you can use to find doctors. You can search by specialty, location and by insurance coverage. If you don't have insurance, there are clinics who offer sliding scales for therapy and fantastic LCADCs who often fit perfectly as many of us are Mentally Ill Chemically Addicted (MICA). There are also LCSW and LPCs. Ask around and compare their rates to copays and remember to check if they offer sliding scales. Look at all your options as long as they have experience at helping bipolars. That is the key.

QUESTIONS FOR YOUR PSYCHIATRIST:

✓ Is depression causing my symptoms?

✓ What will our strategy be for treatment?

✓ Are there any restrictions I need to follow?

✓ Is there any material I can take home?

✓ Are there any side effects with my meds?

✓ Do you have any samples for this med?

Tip Twenty-Three: Preparing for Appointments

It is a smart idea to look at your appointment as an opportunity. Do you have questions? How about writing them down to be your memory? We do this faithfully. (Our memories are horrible!) If you are there for a med check, you have approximately fifteen minutes to jam in a lot of business. Having a list of your concerns and questions for your psychiatrist in advance of your appointment ensures you will get to it. Plant yourself there until every item on your list has been addressed. There is a lot of ground to cover—often more than you realize—which is why the list is a beautiful thing. Doctors love them (unless they are running late!) Having a list of your symptoms gives the doctor a better idea of what's going on. Once they know you have it, they'll want to knock it out which gives you the advantage of getting all your concerns addressed before your time is up. It's a win-win. Memory back-up, check. Leave with all answers, check check. Making the most of your appointment: check check check.

Plus, don't forget your Ziploc of meds. It's handy rather than keeping track of your refills. After your questions have been addressed, you can simply hand over your Ziploc to your doctor. They'll appreciate taking out bottles to check needed refills, especially if you're running short on time.

Tip Twenty-Four: Be Honest

Honesty is always the best policy, and Billy Joel said it best: "is such a lonely word." Omitting things that are embarrassing hurts your recovery. Once you fully trust your doctor, it will be easier to open up and get the help you need. It's almost like choosing to take half of your meds or get half of the sleep you need. To sit with your psychologist, pretend everything is okay and talk about surface issues and dodge painful illness and current behaviors, does us no good. Besides, your psychologist won't have to yawn. (Don't you hate that? Ever want to make up something juicy to wake them up?) Do yourselves a favor and tell them what's really going on. You'll get your money's worth and get the help and feedback you and your illness are craving.

However embarrassing or depressing, our health care circle all needs to know what's going on because behaviors are mood indicators, and our psychiatrists are our mood disorder doctors. Our behaviors not only display our moods, they also indicate how our meds are or are not working. Everyone needs to be in the loop and lying, diminishing the truth or downplaying it only hurts us in the long run. It is a team effort to stay well and at the helm is honesty.

 WENDY:

I used to omit things, especially when I was manic or hypersexual. I never told any professional the antics I was up to, or the real number of men I slept with when manic. Who wants to admit that? I would lower the number or just say they were "dates." It wasn't until I could trust my new psychologist, and had lived long enough with this illness, that I could open up. I have learned to spare my psychiatrist every sordid detail—we have little time anyway—but I certainly tell him highlights of what he needs to know. My psychologist, however, gets full disclosure because we have more time and that's her specialty.

Tip Twenty-Five: Get Samples

Samples are a beautiful thing. We wish we could stock every doctor's office with endless samples of each medication. They rock for a number of reasons. Even for people with insurance, they come in handy more than you would think. Some doctors have them, some don't. It all depends upon your doctor.

If your doctor interacts with pharmaceutical reps, chances are he/she will have samples. Consider yourself lucky if this is your situation. This could come in handy and save you a lot of money. This is particularly helpful when you are just beginning a new medication and don't want to pay for a full prescription until you are certain it works for you. This can also work beautifully when your insurance denies your brand and you are treading water until you can get coverage or find a suitable generic that you respond to. Or, if your insurance will not cover a certain amount of milligrams. There are a number of reasons they come in handy. There is no negative here and we love them.

No matter what your situation, be sure to speak up and ask your doctor if they have samples for XYZ med you are taking as doctors rarely offer unless you ask. If it is a new medication, they may be more apt to reach for them. Be sure to tell them of your situation—if your insurance has denied your brand or if another situation has arisen that makes those samples needed. One starter pack can be worth hundreds of dollars retail. If they ask how many you need, feel free to say "as many as you can spare." Often, we've gotten loaded up on free samples when we needed them.

Remember, this is your health. They might otherwise sit there gaining dust until drug reps make the rounds and can fill them back up. Don't be ashamed and above all: always ask if you need them. Some docs interact with reps more than others. It is time consuming. If you have one of these psychiatrists, you will save a lot of money if you come across the need. That alone can pay for the initial consult you spent out of pocket. It's another reason why we believe in private doctors.

WENDY:

I just used this tip when my insurance wouldn't fill the needed milligrams of one of my meds. Every fall, I gear up for my SAD by taking more of my anti-depressant. My doctor wrote the script for 40mg BID (twice a day). The insurance company denied it. Knowing this was a possibility, my doctor sent me home with two starter packs of my medication. This tied me over until my next visit in case this happened again. Discussing what my insurance will cover for a particular med and having a game plan until next time helps me fill in the gap with samples. I love them. Samples rock!

HONORA:

I tried a new medication not long ago. To fill it would've been expensive even with insurance. My doctor gave me a starter pack to see if it was helpful before I paid the $45 co-pay. The starter pack sample was a month's worth which was enough time to see if it would work for me. They are particularly helpful, I find. Especially when I am trying a brand medication for the first time and it has an expensive co-pay.

Chapter 6

Wellness is rewarded

Tip Twenty-Six: Minimize Stress:

Stress is a huge trigger for bipolars and a leading cause for our episodes. If there was an element we could trace back to all the manic episodes that we have ever had, it would involve stress. While stress is impossible to eradicate, it clearly needs to be managed. It feels like it is starter fluid for a manic flame, blowing it out of control. The two need each other to coexist.

HEALTH PROBLEMS CAUSED OR EXACERBATED BY STRESS:

✓ Depression   ✓ Skin Conditions

✓ Sleep Problems   ✓ Digestive Problems

✓ Pain   ✓ Autoimmune Diseases

✓ Heart Disease

Balance is key and can be elusive. We hate losing speed and slowing down is difficult; we might feel we're losing momentum in accomplishing our goals. There is nothing wrong with occasionally getting out of the fast lane, and it's better for our health. Some common bipolar stress triggers are financial, emotional, work-related, and in our case, when a loved one is manic or depressed. Any of these stressors can cause us to tilt, throwing us out of balance. While we were completing this book, we had to find ways to avoid stress, otherwise we never would have finished. Nor would we have done so without getting manic. There are a wide array of tactics we can use to minimize stress. Everyone is different.

 **WENDY:**

I don't do well with stress and have always known this about myself. When things got too stressful in school, particularly in college, I mentally checked out. I stopped studying; I couldn't handle it. In the work world when I began getting promotions and taking on more responsibilities, I thought my head was going to explode. It was non-stop pressure. Luckily I was downsized, because I don't know if I would've had the courage to leave. After my first major mixed episode, suicide attempts and ECT, I knew I would have to scale the stress way, way back for an indefinite period of time. I have had a stressful job since, but nothing that comes as close. Now that I know the link between stress and mania, I don't dare put myself in that situation. The first stress diffuser that helped me was exercise. I have never felt anything like it for my mind and body since. Ten years later, I began experiencing higher professional stress again and quickly learned I needed to find strategies to cope with stress mentally.

The second, and most recent, stress diffuser has been meditation. Some people still look at me funny. I, too, always thought meditation was for kooks. Still, in a desperate attempt to find ways to calm my mind, I came upon a Twitter frenzy announcing a free twenty-one-day meditation series with Oprah and Deepak Chopra. To my surprise, it worked on the first day. I was so relaxed and saw images. It feels like a minute goes by when in reality, it is ten. I have been doing it ever since and mornings when I don't start off with it feel wrong. It is really calming and has made a huge impact on reducing stress in my life.

REDUCE YOUR STRESS:

- ◆ Develop a Routine
- ◆ Listen to calming music
- ◆ Take a walk
- ◆ Exercise

- ◆ Call a friend
- ◆ Meditate
- ◆ Take a drive
- ◆ Observe nature

This is probably my number one stress reducer; exercise would be my number two.

One thing I do know: mania loves stress.

 HONORA:

Prior to being diagnosed, I was constantly under pressure. Right out of college, I was a young woman trying to make it in the very male-dominated stockbroker business. In that industry, they test you to see if you're worthy of their status. To say it's stressful is an understatement. It was almost as stressful as being a mom.

Today, my medications and therapy with my doctor have made a world of a difference. I feel as though I am able to concentrate and put into perspective the thoughts that enter my brain. Rarely am I racing at a speed I cannot catch up to.

I have a few tactics which help reduce my stress. The trick is to recognize I am getting stressed before it takes over. Even in situations on high stress, I have ways of coping and pulling back when I realize it is making me too speedy. I can spend extra time on our balcony in nature, listening to music, take a little time away from my work or take a drive by the ocean. We can't get rid of stress. Life is stressful! But we can think of ways to reduce it.

Tip Twenty-Seven: Get Moving

There isn't one negative to exercising and there are more positives than you may realize. The physical benefits from exercising are obvious, but we tend to forget about all the mental aspects. Sure, there is a positive by-product from getting fit physically; it boosts our self-esteem, confidence and helps our depression (because we look better). A great number of us are on anti-psychotics and/or anti-convulsants and these types of medications cause weight gain. Weight gain translates to added depression. Several years ago, we went on anti-psychotics and are *still* battling the weight we packed on. Sigh.

Another major benefit to exercise is the mental aspect. Exercise increases the body's naturally produced dopamine, a chemical that's in short supply for most bipolars. There are a few ways, in addition to medication, to get this in to our brains. One is exercise, another is laughter, and yet another is sex. If we could laugh at funny movies when depressed, problem solved. If we could all solve our problems with tons of sex, fantastic! The truth is, getting motivated to do even the simplest of physical activities is difficult, if not impossible, when we are depressed. None of the above is happening, let alone when we are severely depressed. Moving often feels impossible and exercise is the last thing we feel like doing. We need it, but we feel we can't move. We crave it, but our brains

A recent National Health and Nutrition survey found that physically active people were half as likely to be depressed.

DID YOU KNOW? EXERCISE ALSO HELPS:

♦ Reduce depression

♦ Reduce blood pressure

♦ Reduce cholesterol levels

♦ Reduce risk of certain cancers

stop us from getting what we need. If our medications are not holding us, it will be hard to get off the couch, out of bed, perhaps out of our homes at all. This is the great problem. We can exercise when we feel well, but the crucial time we need it is exactly when we are the least apt to do it.

It would be horrible, fake advice to simply say "get out there and do it anyway." We are realists. Do the best you can. Besides having a routine, enlist help. It could be a person you meet at the gym, a friend for walks, or family member helping you with your goal. Without help, exercise can be tough. This has been, hands down, the greatest source of difficulty. Enlisting the help of an exercise buddy has been our method for success.

 WENDY:

When I exercise regularly I am in the best mental shape. It does everything the doctors say. My anxieties and depression are drastically reduced and I feel better about myself. There is something empowering about taking positive steps for your health; especially when it extends to your mental well-being.

Lately, I have fallen off the wagon. You don't realize how much your routine helps you until you break it. I know it typically takes another person to help motivate me to exercise. My desk chair cushion is one of the warmest places in our house. Just ask the cats!

HONORA:

These days I talk about walking, I talk the talk, but I need to focus on walking the walk. This is an area where I could use improvement. When the winter comes, I barely like to go outside. This is when I get the least amount of exercise as I go into winter hibernation like the bears.

Tip Twenty-Eight: Try Vitamins

Vitamins can be beneficial. They are relatively harmless and there are many vitamins on the market that people with bipolar disorder take. We follow the general trend here. While some research indicates the same effect as placebos, another test for that same vitamin could show a 50% or higher positive effect. With little consistency, this leaves some of the medical community and consumers skeptical.

Before taking a particular vitamin, we need to remember we are sensitive creatures. Whatever we take, vitamin or herb, affects our chemistry. Before we wrote this book, we thought, "it's just a vitamin. What harm could it do?" Now our eyes are open. They'll remain open as additions to our wellness as studies continue to be done.

The most common and therefore notable ones are: B-Complex, Omega Fish Oil, Vitamin D and St. John's Wort. It is helpful to read medical websites and those niched to bipolar disorder specifically. Note that websites such as WebMD and various others don't specifically address the effects on bipolars. We have found a lot of useful information on Psych

Central; just type "vitamins" into the search box for a host of education information. There are updated books that are very comprehensive, such as *Bipolar for Dummies: 2nd Edition.*

St. John's Wort, an herb, was all the buzz in the U.S. in the nineties; yet now we don't hear about it as much. As it turns out, St. John's Wort has the potential to take you out of depression and into mania. Be careful. It works like an anti-depressant, just like any that can do that to us. We have had that experience with anti-depressants and it is the same principle. As always, consult your doctor as with any vitamins, to make sure it won't disrupt your regimen or mood.

Vitamins can be helpful for a number of reasons and reading up on them can help. We write our questions down and bring them to our psychiatrist to discuss it. Vitamins can get expensive, especially if you are taking several, so this way our doctor lets us know if the vitamin has a negative interaction before we spend the money.

> One side effect of St. John's Wort is it can launch mania and it interacts with various medications, notably birth control.

 **WENDY:**

I had foot surgery a few years ago and began taking Vitamin D post-op at the suggestion of my surgeon. At checkups, he said I was healing ahead of schedule and this has been the main reason I am a believer in vitamins. (I was taking 1000 mg, twice his recommended amount.) I believe Vitamin D contributed to this and continue to take it to this day.

I am willing to try anything, but I do my research. Combing medical websites, articles and journals, I found some disagreement over the effectiveness of vitamins. The trend among vitamin research overall is inconsistency, I'm afraid. I will make my own conclusions, but I do know there is something to vitamins and their benefits. There are promising studies with Omega Fish oils and depression, but they hovered around fifty/fifty efficacy. Honora has had great success with taking B12-Complex three times a day. I noticed a change in her and was amazed to find out it wasn't a pharmaceutical! Now we both take Omega Fish Oils and B12 Complex faithfully.

I'm not looking for a miracle worker—that's a Philosophy moisturizer. I simply have high hopes for vitamins and feel they're an often overlooked part of wellness.

VITAMINS AND YOU

- ◆ Consult your doctor
- ◆ Research through reputable sites and books
- ◆ Read labels to know what you are getting.
- ◆ Give it time before giving up
- ◆ Purchase small quantities

 HONORA:

My energy level was really low, and my doctor suggested I take B12-Complex. Initially, I tried the once-a-day variety, but did not notice a difference. I went to Walgreen's and found they had a B12-complex where you take six a day. I thought I would try taking two in the morning, two in the afternoon, and two in the evening, instead of one at nighttime. It made all the difference in the world! I felt as though I had a constant infusion of energy throughout the day. Try it and see if the same goes for you. Of course, clear it with your doctor. If they give you the green light, my advice is try the non-extended release first. If you take meds a few times a day, it will be easy to add them to your pill tray.

Tip Twenty-Nine: Aromatherapy

Aromatherapy is often overlooked, yet so simple to add as part of your wellness solution. And it's one of the most fun! We use it all the time between burning candles and lighting incense, to splashing shower oils and spraying perfumes. What do we know about aromatherapy and our brains? To answer this, we had to do some research.

The two basic elements to aromatherapy are the influence of aroma on the brain—notably the limbic system through the olfactory system—and the other is the pharmacological effects of the oils. The precise knowledge of the synergy between the body and aromatic oils is claimed by aroma therapists. Still, no one knows the exact efficacy of aromatherapy. There have been a few clinical studies of aromatherapy in combination with other techniques that show positive effects. Also, since olfactory is the strongest sense, it would stand to reason there is something to this.

When we spoke of aromatherapy to our psychiatrist, to describe how it made us feel, he immediately went right in to talking about the Roman baths. He said it was believed the salts used could have improved their mood. Can you imagine? The ancient Romans were brilliant. Where do we sign up?

You might try scented candles, oils, perfumes or incense. Whatever floats your boat: go for it! We constantly experiment, incense being our latest go to smell. Lemongrass and lavender are our favorites.

> Ancient Roman art dates aromatherapy
> back to 2650 B.C.
> They used it during healing rituals
> to calm patients.

 **WENDY:**

I now include aromatherapy in every article I write on wellness. Often, we focus on the big ticket items to stay well and forget about the little ones in between that make us happy. The nose knows and this goes a long way. Even while I write, I keep a candle lit at my desk. It creates a relaxing atmosphere. (Plus, the cat box is in the office, so it helps diffuse the smell!)

My mom recently went to Asia and brought us back some treats. Besides the deep green, marble Buddha, she brought us lemongrass incense cones that smell heavenly. We savored them. That is what started us on our incense kick. (In the past, neither one of us were fans of incense. It reminded us of college parties that used to spin our heads!) All it took to change our minds were these little cones from Asia. Now we are hooked and have stumbled upon the world of incense. We already ordered and received more lemongrass incense through Amazon. com from Thailand; though we've decided they are definitely imposters.

 ## HONORA:

A favorite trick of mine is to spray my favorite perfume or cologne every day. Even if I am not going anywhere, I put it on. My favorites are Clarins and Dolce and Gabanna Light Blue. I always feel better about myself with my favorite perfume on. It's one of my quickest fixes for a lift. Chances are your loved one will compliment you, too, so it's a win-win. I keep several small bottles of lavender and verbena in the shower and splash that on myself too. I am all about smells.

Ancient Romans used oils in their world famous baths.

•

Ancient Greeks were the first to use aromatherapy medicinally.

•

Ancient Chinese used them in acupuncture and massage.

•

Europeans embraced oils by mixing them to make perfumes.

Tip Thirty: Candles Set the Mind

We love candles and anything that helps calm us. If you are working with a tight budget, try buying small tea lights. They are far less expensive than the big candles and achieve the same effect. Each lasts approximately three hours, which is plenty of time to send a message of calm to your brain and set the stage of peace.

We light candles inside and outside on the patio. It creates a peaceful and calming sanctuary for us. Nighttime is usually when we are the most revved up and peaceful lighting is a logical solution. It transitions us from bright light to low light to a dark bedroom. We need all the help we can get.

Tea lights are handy because they extinguish in less than three hours. If you opt for a larger candle, try the ones in glass. Both of these are safer in case you doze off. Either way, blow them out *before* you get sleepy. No candle is worth your house.

Tip Thirty-One: Shower Power

This is one of our quickest tips: shower! It may sound basic, but sometimes it slips our mind as one of the fastest things we can do to make ourselves feel better. Oh, does it feel good!

When we are depressed—as we all know—it causes our hygiene to take a nose dive. It's one of the first things we notice about ourselves and in each other. It's one of the fastest ways to gauge our moods. Typically, we both lean towards depression rather than mania, and when we're feeling low self-care becomes a chore rather than routine.

The impact that a hot shower has on our moods never ceases to amaze us, as if we are rediscovering this each time we do it. Most people shower in the morning, each day before work, like clockwork. It's not a thought or a fight to do so. Depression causes you to battle hygiene. To the outside world, this may seem like laziness. For those of us with bipolar disorder, going without showers while depressed makes perfect sense.

We will go days without showering. Typically it's because of depression while occasionally it's a lack of energy. (This could still be a slick patch of milder depression.) Then we take one and remember it not only feels good, but we feel better that we did it. It can be the biggest achievement for the day if we are down enough. In the spring and summer, we don't give showering a second thought. When we are experiencing SAD, in the fall and winter, that's when the challenge comes. We always feel so good afterwards that it leaves us wondering why we don't take more. That's the power of a shower.

 WENDY:

When I was working my last nine to five job, I showered every morning. I felt normal, like I had joined the human race! Now that I write full-time, I don't have to shower first thing in the morning or at all. It doesn't matter what I look like sitting in front of my computer. I often wonder though, if I jumped in the shower earlier, would I be more productive? But there's something about getting my body wet that early that I find unappealing. In fact, I think there's nothing worse than waking up and showering right away. When I did though, it felt great. Honora and I always joke that in the winter, if we didn't have social events and appointments, we would hardly ever shower. When my hair hurts, it's my signal that it's time to jump in!

HONORA:

As a child, my parents used to have to pay me a quarter to take a shower. I would sit in the tub with the shower on. Sometimes I still do this and it feels comforting. I do feel better when I shower; Wendy and I always marvel at how much better we feel. We always put it on our mental to do list: take more showers. Can you imagine how good we'd feel if we took them every day? We can always tell where we are at mentally by how many we are taking per week. Once I'm in, I love it. I use wonderful bath gels and the best smelling shampoos and conditioners. It is one thing we splurge on.

Tip Thirty-Two: Reward Yourself

If you have a bad habit to quit or high hurdle to surmount, try setting a goal with a reward at the end of the rainbow. For example, if you set a financial reward for no longer drinking or smoking, you will be more likely to achieve it. This was actually an idea given to us by a couple who had quit smoking, saved the money they would've spent on cigarettes, and used it to go on a trip. We recommend that you begin with tackling the goal that is currently impeding upon your wellness. This is the perfect place to start!

As we write this book, we have planned a trip as a reward. We are of the mentality that we need a carrot at the end of our sticks. When we were single our rewards varied. One of us would reward ourselves for working hard by going to a movie, the other with going to dinner with a friend. Not everyone is the same. When we began writing we started off small. In the beginning once we finished a few chapters, we would go out to dinner and felt good about our reward.

Our mental health is fragile, like a piece of china, and we have to protect it any way we can. To do that, the reward system is beautiful.

 WENDY:

When I quit smoking, I vowed I would buy myself something that cost the same as three months' worth of cigarettes. I saved for three months—the exact amount I would've spent on cigarettes—and voila: I bought my first generation iPod. I'd also recommend the bigger the goal, the greater reward. It's a great incentive and it works. Small goals with small rewards can be just as effective as achieving big goals with big rewards. In fact, they can be your stepping stones to help you with the big ones.

 HONORA:

This tip can be as fun as you make it. There's nothing like the feeling of accomplishing what's on my to-do list and after a week or two, making an iTunes mix or get a new pair of jeans in a month.

Chapter 7

create
your life

Tip Thirty-Three: Find Your Creative Edge

Are you a woodworker? Do you love painting? Are you a closet poet? Don't forget amidst the things we all do on a daily basis—the daily grind—to allow yourself the time for creative play. Inside most bipolars is an artist of some type. Do you love photography? You don't have to set up a studio and run a business. But dammit, grab your camera and get out there. You won't have a picture to mount if you're sitting on your couch.

 WENDY:

I used to work a nine-to-five job that didn't suit my personality. I needed it for the benefits, paycheck and stability, but it wasn't a fit. It was a Fortune 500 company that wanted numbers, numbers and yet greater numbers from us. You always felt like if you didn't produce, someone else could walk through the door, get trained and be hired to do your job. I was stressed, bored and felt trapped.

Mainly, my creative side took a hit and was stuffed away. In lieu of writing or anything creative, I spent endless hours at a desk. We do what we have to do to survive. But I knew I needed a hobby to balance my stress. My mom had been pushing me to take a class and I'd brushed her off for a long time; although I loved her delightfully positive and quirky, artistic friend Alison. Alison was teaching the class and had it been anyone else, anyone less enthusiastic, that I didn't already know, I might not have ever gone. I was so afraid of doing something outside my comfort zone! Ultimately, I became more afraid of getting so far from myself I could never get the old, creative Wendy back. Like my light would completely be eaten up by my brown office, depressing metal desk and the berber carpet in my apartment. Everything felt drab and dark at that point in my life. Out of desperation, I conceded.

Every Wednesday after work I ran home, changed into grubby clothes and did pottery for two hours. I made no masterpieces by any stretch of the imagination, but it was a nice escape. I had a lot of pottery to give at family and friends' birthdays and Christmas time which saved me a lot of money. Though years later I am cringing at the embarrassing, lopsided creatures hiding in corners of loved ones houses' everywhere!

These wonderful women in my class each week provided a fantastic, creative, much needed diversion from the everyday duldrums of life. It was social, which is always the best aspect of any group hobby for me. I am typically introverted, so any activity that forces me to socialize is a huge plus. I believe pottery opened the floodgates to my writing career, as I began writing and haven't stopped yet.

 HONORA:

In this area, Wendy and I couldn't be more different. I have always been the mathematical type. Being a stock broker, I played the numbers game until my thirties. If there was any creativity in me, I certainly didn't know it. Now my life is completely different; I probably couldn't add ten plus ten if I tried! Ah, the cognitive joys of having bipolar disorder. It comes with the territory.

Today, I am a writer and an editor. I feel like I have a purpose in life; the sense of self-worth I have now is because of what I have accomplished so far. And I am just beginning! I never imagined I'd ever have such an amazing, artistic outlet and career.

Tip Thirty-Four: Start Something

Ask yourself what you enjoy doing. Do you enjoy photography or dancing? Wish you had company for weekend trips? Think back to what you loved when you were younger. Did you go camping and hiking with your parents and perhaps you miss it? Did you always have a camera in your hand in high school? Maybe you once danced up a storm and long to find a partner to learn new steps? Try pulling out old photo albums to remember what made you happy when you were younger. You could look in your local paper to jog your memory for ideas, too.

Once you know what that something is you have a few options. You can do what we did which is to start a group on Meetup.com. Although there is a small monthly charge, it is the fastest way to form a group as using the internet essentially finds people for you. You will have an instant support group of people who share your same passion. It grows and grows with time. In our first year, we had less than fifty people in our writers group. Three years later, we have two hundred and fifty people! At each meeting, there is a new person and this makes for an evolving, interesting mix of people. Variety is the spice of life!

Another way to start your group is to put the feelers out by emailing a group of friends. This way is totally free, but may take longer to build. This could work if your interest is best experienced in smaller numbers and common. For example, maybe you are looking to have a consistent walking club. Or maybe you'd like one or two people to work on classic cars with or make jewelry. Start with someone who has a positive energy that you'd like to spend time with. Ideally, you have a friend that shares a love you do. Starting a club is easy. It's the advertising, costs, meeting scheduling, momentum and keeping the group together you'll need to focus on.

Also, many newspapers have an almanac section and will advertise your group's meeting free of charge. Our writers group meets in libraries and cafes. Your group could be recruited, maintained and meet for free or nominally. Voila! Who says every support group has to be about mental health? Get out there and have some fun!

 **WENDY:**

One of the greatest joys of my writing career has been to share my passion. As corny as this sounds, it is absolutely true. This came true when I co-founded The Red Bank Writers Group with Honora, and we are still going strong today.

I got the idea to start our writers group after attending someone else's group. It was far away and I wanted the same type group locally. It has proved to be not only a wonderful creative source, it's a human experience; this is a far cry from being alone in my apartment writing. I'm thrilled to be making new friends, sharing, exchanging resources and feeling energized every time we meet. It has been one of my greatest joys in the past few years. I get hope from my fellow writers and we cheer each other on. The support is a huge part in my life.

Tip Thirty-Five: Get Out & Have Fun!

There are many things you can do to get out and enjoy life. Our favorite things to do are: going to the movies, concerts and traveling. If price is a major consideration, and it is for many of us, you may have to get creative. Our main message, though, is to get out. For those bipolars who are frequently more depressed, like us, this is often easier said than done. We hope you have a friend who can help you get out of the house. We are fortunate that we have each other. Usually one of us can pull the other out the door. However, when we are both down, having each other sometimes still isn't enough.

When we were single we did things alone. If you have the beauty of independence, there are some perks and the freedom to do what you want when you want is one of them. We have found some of our finest moments in the days, weeks and months when were alone. Going to the movies was the perfect thing to do alone. It is dark and you can make an easy entrance and escape. It is liberating. We could see what movies we wanted, when we wanted and it didn't matter what time it was— even a late show.

With concerts, we have to be more selective because even decent seats at our little community theater have gotten pretty expensive. Still, it is important to pay attention to the arts you love and finding a way to get out. Consider it a reward for working hard.

For travel, if you have to think budget, realize your current situation will not always be your future one. Case in point: we went on our first cruise in 2013. If we always believed we would be broke writers—we would have been okay with camping—but we never would have dreamed about cruises. Now we are about to embark on our second, which will be our honeymoon. And to think: it all began with a hand-me-down tent! Though we will always be happy, whether in a tent, hotel room or on a cruise, we must admit, beds are more comfortable. But we will always camp. The campfires are relaxing, and we get a lot of work done there too!

 WENDY:

I am a huge movie fiend. I went every few weeks when I was single. Sometimes I would go with my mom or a friend; more often than not, though, I went alone and didn't mind. I enjoyed going to whichever movie I wanted to see at whatever time. I could eat all the popcorn and candy I wanted and didn't have to monitor myself in the presence of my date. (One date made a comment about how I used to eat popcorn by the handful!) When I was stressed, it was my quickest go-to fix to get outside of myself for two hours.

 HONORA:

When I met Wendy we began camping with her friends a couple of times a year. We longed for the silence and beauty of nature by ourselves and thus began traveling and camping at national parks in PA, NJ, and VA. I get my best work done (editing, not writing) when we're in the woods. There is no electricity, cell phones or television to distract me.

Something funny happens on every trip. On our last one, we took great strides to protect our food from raccoons by bringing it into the cabin only to have a mouse eat it! And that little critter made noise like a bear! It may as well have been one; we were terrified. Who knew something so small could make so much noise?

Tip Thirty-Six: Volunteer

The beautiful thing about volunteering is you are not only helping a cause, you are helping yourself. You will get outside yourself and realize there are people worse off than you. It's the same principle as the phone calls, but better. You are forced to get out in to the world and leave your home. This helps combat depression. Plus, making a difference gives you an infusion of purpose and makes you feel needed in this world.

 WENDY:

There was a time I was depressed off and on for two years. An acquaintance announced they needed help at a local market for an hour a few days a week packing crates for their truck that went to NYC. I did it every week for just over a year and afterwards went to a DBSA meeting. It gave me purpose during a time when I was floating out there feeling like no one needed me, and I wanted to die. I felt these people who were homeless in NYC needed the food I was helping to pack, and it gave me a sense that my life was worthwhile. Everyone can make a difference. Often it takes a natural disaster to open our eyes, but helping anyone in need on the day to day makes for a better world.

Tip Thirty-Seven: Writing and Journaling

Writing of any type opens you up. It gets down your feelings—which could be part of the process of healing—for bipolars or anyone. Some hand write, some type. We suggest you hand write for emotion. It's amazing what comes out. Everyone has their method, but the important part is not to deny you this path, regardless of your occupation or interests.

Even if you are not into writing, per se, keeping a journal, writing poems, writing letters and even writing long emails to friends, can be very therapeutic. There is discovery when pen hits paper, or when fingers hit the keys.

In our Red Bank Writers Group we have a myriad of writers. The only thing we have in common is we like to write. We have various motivations for it, but the common thread is we do it because it feels good. To some it feels right, a click, "this is what I should be doing with my life." Some go to workshops in the woods, some go back to school. Some simply carve out ten minutes of their busy day to write anything. For some it is a living. What we have in common is that it brings a desired result inside us. That is what we wish for you. It can be as therapeutic for someone with a mental illness, if not more, than for someone who is writing for the love of it. In many ways, it is one in the same.

 WENDY:

I used to have a psychiatrist who asked me to journal and turn it in to her every week. It proved effective not only for her to know where I was at mentally; it helped me to get out my feelings. Recently, I've returned to this practice and begin the day this way. I wake up and with my coffee, get it all out. I just spill my fears and anxieties on paper. I believe it helps me clear my mind and reduce my anxiety. There is a book called *The Artist's Way* and it has a practice called "The Morning Pages." This is where I first learned about it.

 HONORA:

I have always kept those little notebooks in my purse. Not only will you find my grocery list in there, but you can also find poems, notes, and/or personal sentiments in there. I have been keeping these "little journals" for years. I even record my moods, how I'm feeling, up or down.

I usually don't write for more than five to ten minutes at a time; I find it easier and more manageable this way. Besides, it's what you write that matters, not that it's a novel. And it's fun to look back and see how far I've come.

> If you're not into journaling,
> try handwriting a few mornings.
> You may find you uncover a few things
> that are blocking you.
> Even people who aren't writers
> suffer from blocks.

Chapter 8

Organization is the key to success

Tip Thirty-Eight: Do Your Research

Research is knowledge and knowledge is power. Never has this rung more true than when staying on top of your illness. It is good practice to stay current with bipolar websites, medical journals, periodicals and up-to-date blogs. This is one area we, and many newly diagnosed bipolars, lack at the onset.

All of this combined is part of the wellness puzzle; we put these pieces together to stay on top of our game. It is constantly changing and evolving as grants are given, our government is voting and studies are done. Research is a huge piece. The laws are finally changing which affects us enormously.

The good news is there are websites that make it very easy for us to learn. They are: NAMI (National Alliance on Mental Illness), DBSA (Depression and Bipolar Support Alliance), NIMH (National Institute of Mental Health), SAMSHA (Substance Abuse and Mental Health Services Administration), Mayo Clinic, APA (American Psychiatric Association), International Bipolar Foundation (IBPF) and MHA (Mental Health America). They lead the way and offer excellent summaries of what is going on in the bipolar world. We also like *BP Magazine*, BPHope.com, *PsychCentral.com* and *HealthyPlace.com*.

RESEARCH TIPS:

✓ Get educated through www.nami.org and www.dbsa.org.

✓ Stay current through periodicals and up-to-date blogs.

✓ Read www.psychiatry.org and www.nimh.nih.gov.

Be sure to look at the source and assess the study with a discerning eye. Was it a sample of ten people or a hundred? Were the findings by a drug company or professors at a university study? Was the drug in pre-trial testing while trying to receive FDA approval? These are the first questions we pay attention to and our psychiatrist has interesting input. It's important to stay on top of our illness and the research is ever changing.

 WENDY:

When I was first diagnosed, I could care less about research. I couldn't get over my diagnosis, let alone jump in and learn what was going on. After a decade, I began to read about my illness. Since then, I've paid more and more attention to research and the latest news about bipolar disorder. I have alerts set up for two major national newspapers on mental illness and read *Bipolar Magazine*. I sift through the medical journals and find pearls which I apply to my life. The American Psychiatric Association is my recent favorite: *www.psychiatry.org*. To find them, go to their site, click on the "publications" tab, type "bipolar" and scroll to "psychiatry online." There are over four thousand published articles. It is the greatest collection we have seen. National Institute of Health's NIMH *www.nimh.nih.gov* has amassed a top collection of bipolar research, too. Organizations such as these make it easy to stay on top of research with their sites that catalogue them for you.

GET INVOLVED! HOW?

- ◆ Become part of the bipolar community: volunteer and advocate.
- ◆ Follow blogs and online sites such as: Psych Central, Healthy Place & BPHope.com.
- ◆ Tweet. Find other bipolars who give hope, inspire & make you laugh.
- ◆ Read periodicals such as *BP Magazine*.
- ◆ Get connected so you won't feel alone.
- ◆ Go to NAMI, DBSA, NIMH, SAMSHA, IBPF & MHA websites to learn.

 HONORA:

I may read as many as twenty online papers, sources and websites a day. The latest news is something I seem to crave. Wendy calls me a news media junkie, which I find funny, but it is true. I was accustomed to reading five or six newspapers each morning for my job as a stock broker; it's a habit that started in my early twenties. Today, I remain a voracious reader.

You may have noticed that mental illness stories are all over the media these days. Unfortunately, many of it is degrading and downright inaccurate. It is frustrating to be portrayed in a negative light. Mainstream media, as far as I'm concerned, is misleading the public.

What can we do? Well, for starters, if it makes you feel discouraged and defeated, avoid it like the plague. There are other electronic media and television and radio outlets that are more sympathetic to our cause (NAMI, DBSA, MHA, IBPF and NIMH to name a few.) Another recommendation is to educate yourself on the facts about our disease. This way, we are able to plant the seeds of authentic information to our friends and family. And slowly this can improve the perception of our illness.

Tip Thirty-Nine: Be Proactive

Tackling bipolar disorder is like any sport. The best offense is a good defense. To us, this equates to being proactive. It's similar to living with diabetes. You have to monitor yourself, your intake, your medicine, and it is best controlled proactively versus reactively. If you're diabetic you watch your sugar before you go into shock; similarly, if you're bipolar, it's wise to get proper sleep, take your meds and keep stress to a minimum before you get manic or depressed. This also means getting in to see our doc when we need to fine tune our meds.

If any of these are neglected, our illness will come on full force. There goes the offense and proactivity! Then it's time to scramble and prepare for crash landings. We try hard every day to stay on top of our illness and do everything we can to the best of our abilities. Lightning will strike, but it helps if you are not in the water. It's far easier in the long run to do what you are supposed to do than fall behind and be prime for depression or mania to take hold of you.

 WENDY:

Late summer, I automatically make an appointment with my psychiatrist in anticipation of my mood drop-off in early fall. It has become like clockwork. We fine tune my meds, notably my anti-depressant, before I crash. It helps lower my dip. This winter I am trying two different tactics. For one, I am taking the B12-Complex vitamin Honora swears by. (I am determined to not go down without a fight.) We also just bought a 10,000 lux, 5000 kelvin, white light, light box. I can't wait to try it out! If it works, it could be the biggest part of combating my SAD yet. It doesn't work for everyone, but I hope it does for me.

Each year I try to add another wellness tip to my arsenal. I like the idea that I am being proactive, not reactive. It makes me feel I'm doing everything in my power to keep at a level playing field.

 HONORA:

I am a rapid cycler. My moods can shift with the wind. As the years have gone by, I have gotten better at identifying when I feel myself taking off or crashing. And it doesn't take much. Missing my meds once or restless sleep for a couple of days and I am off to the races.

It's difficult when things can change on a dime, but I am much better at taking action today. When everyone is out trick or treating, I am on my psychiatrist's couch discussing with him my impending annual winter crash. We increase my anti-depressant, lower a medication that can make me foggy during the day and this year, I am going to suggest to him a medication I have researched on the internet. It may help me with my energy.

You see, all these things that I do today, I never did years ago. I allowed myself to fall in to such a suicidal seasonal depression without so much as calling anyone for help. Today, I feel like I am in charge and in control of my illness. I haven't been successful in completely eliminating my winter depression, but I am *trying* to fight it today. It's not an option to just live with the suffering from between Thanksgiving through March.

Tip Forty: Make To Do Lists

You know what they say: organization is the key to success. This is as true for our illness as it is for life in general. Our tip is to start a "To-Do" list as soon as you get anxious about all that you need to do. Make them several times a week, or as often as you get anxious. It lifts the anxiety out of your brain, onto paper and gives us a sense of accomplishment. The key is referring back to your list, experimenting and making long-term goals that will take time to complete. Above all, be patient with yourself. To become organized takes practice and no one gets there overnight.

We do have a mood disorder and some days we ignore them altogether. We may not be in the mood to accomplish any of it. Then, we may make a call or do a small chore from the list. It is not an all or nothing thing. The main thing we have learned is to use these lists as motivation. They are our reference, our memories and when we do check them off, there is a genuine sense of achievement.

GET ORGANIZED!

- ◆ Make Lists.
- ◆ Identify and separate short vs. long term goals.
- ◆ Carry it with you.
- ◆ Realize it's okay not to complete them.
- ◆ Use your phone's "notes" section.
- ◆ Reward yourself for tasks accomplished.

 **WENDY:**

I am an incessant list-maker. My lists are not only helpful for my less than stellar memory, they give me a sense of accomplishment when I check those babies off. If I'm in a meeting or a waiting room at a doctor's office, I might make use of my time by pulling out my notebook. If I'm at my desk, it's the Post-It method. I am constantly making lists wherever I am. I've even begun using the "notes" section on my iPhone for lists. My phone helps in a pinch. If we never write our lists down, they zip out of our brains; we tend to forget everything! This is either due to cognitive impairment from our illness, meds or both. It could also be a splash of old age creeping up. Whatever the case, our lists have our back.

 HONORA:

My notebook is my memory backup. I keep it in my purse and it has a spot right next to my trusty pill box. Without fail, you can always find these two things on me at any given time. I even keep my pen hooked in to the binder because you know pens have a way of disappearing. This is the same notebook I use to journal in. It's super convenient to have my notes and personal writings together. When I am done with the notebook, I even date them with a sharpie and keep them in my desk. My notebooks go back to 2006!

Tip Forty-One: Stick to a Routine

Routines save lives. However, if there is one thing that seems boring, it is the word routine. People with bipolar disorder *loathe* routines. The mere thought of it may conjure up sour milk. Yet, if you incorporate routine into your day, previously missed medication can be corrected, and once-forgotten meds can rescue you from impending episodes. This could end up saving your life. Routines also encourage regular sleep which also helps control mania. There is no negative to living within a routine. Work helps regulate this pattern if the bipolar is able.

Our doctor equates bipolars taking meds as part of a routine with the methodical checks they do on airplanes to clear before flight. Without this series of mechanical checks, there could be a problem. In the worst case, the plane could conceivably crash. We know all about crashes and the routines can make all the difference.

It is no different for bipolars. If we fail to take our medications or get our sleep, we are omitting these checks and it will catch up with us. However, if we implement and stick to some form of a routine, we are less likely to make a mistake and more likely to be even.

 WENDY:

I did my all-time best when I waitressed for five years. It was my best stretch of health ever. I firmly believe this was because of my set way of life. Now, I work from home and establishing a work routing has been difficult. When you leave the house to work, it's much easier because you are forced to clock in.

Sometimes creating your own routine takes time to get the kinks out, but it definitely has its benefits. My sleep pattern has been pretty consistent over the last eight years. I try to stay close to my circadian rhythm, as it is best for keeping me on routine.

Tip Forty-Two: Put on Your Bipolar Glasses

We've made many decisions in our lives and each one affects our wellness; our illness is always in the equation. We've begun to refer to it as using our "bipolar glasses." There are many times when we put our bipolar glasses on to make our choices. They involve decisions about jobs, sleep, relationships and overall good living choices.

Life is far from perfect. The best you can do is consider stimuli of noise and light and become aware of decisions that affect your sleep and well-being. Before you sign the lease or buy the house, our advice is to put on your bipolar glasses and think of your health. Before you take the job or jump into the relationship, ask yourself, is this a wise choice? Or, can I handle the stress of this job?

PUT ON YOUR BIPOLAR GLASSES AND ASK YOURSELF:

 ♦ Will this choice be a positive or negative one?
 ♦ How will this choice affect my mental health?
 ♦ Is this relationship a positive or negative influence on my mental illness?
 ♦ Is this job, situation, etc. worth my mental health?

 **WENDY:**

In the past, I never used my bipolar glasses to filter any decisions I made. I was still grappling with accepting my illness, taking meds and freaking out over how my life had forever changed. Even in my late twenties, decisions weren't made based on anything besides my wants. This meant jobs, relationships, apartments, you name it. Once I learned to put my health first, I realized I had to make every major and some minor decisions with my illness in mind.

Now, my glasses are on and wellness is at an all-time high. I'm not immune to mania or depression, but I'm able to handle more than I used to. Life is far better today than it ever has been. For that, I have to thank my bipolar glasses. They keep it real.

 **HONORA:**

Until a few years after my diagnosis—in my early thirties—I wasn't paying attention to how the choices I made affected my illness. I also never thought about my sleep or how decisions in my personal life could influence my disease. These were the furthest things from my mind.

Today, I'm learning to think of my wellness first. For example, I count back nine hours to know when I must go to bed—and stick to it! I make healthier eating choices, too. I try to minimize stress and ask for help when I need it. I know how to look through the lenses of my "bipolar glasses" and make clear decisions that positively affect me.

WHEN CHOOSING WHERE TO SLEEP:

- Listen for neighbor's evening noise level before you sign or buy.
- Choose the quietest bedroom. It's time to get selfish for your health!
- Place bed away from window.
- Choose the darkest A.M. light bedroom.

Chapter 9

SUNSHINE

Tip Forty-Three: Consider the Summer Sun

Doesn't the sun feel good? We live near the beach and the summer is our favorite time of the year. Vitamin D is created naturally by the body in response to exposure to sunlight. It doesn't take much, so be careful. The summers we have experienced more mania were not coincidentally the summers we spent more days at the beach. Who knew?

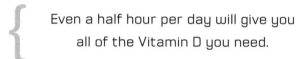

{ Even a half hour per day will give you all of the Vitamin D you need. }

We have figured out a plan that works well for us. Most days we are inside writing. Those days of carefree living at the beach are long gone! When we do go, we sit under an umbrella that blocks the UVA/UVB rays for the majority of the time. We allow ourselves some sun, but we are very careful.

 WENDY:

I've had two summers where I was more manic than the others. We were all scratching our heads to figure it out. Sure I was stressed out from the radio tour, but I was managing my sleep. Then my psychologist looked at my tan and asked if I had been going to the beach a lot. I gulped. Was I in trouble?

It turns out I was. It had to be pointed out to me by my very intelligent psychologist that too much sun can induce mania. Had she not mentioned this, I might never have known. Then she went on to explain how your body only needs thirty minutes and if you get more than that you run the risk of getting manic. Even if you're not looking directly at the sun. Who knew?

 HONORA:

I love the beach! We grew up going to the beach every summer day as a kid. Years ago there wasn't an emphasis on sunblock or much analysis done about time spent in the sun. (I spent all day in and out of the ocean. We swam like fish!) As a result, of all the studies regarding the dangers of getting too much sun, we have tried to minimize our exposure. And to prevent skin cancer, too.

No doubt, it can be frustrating the delicate balance we must achieve treating our bipolar disorder and having fun, but it is doable. We sit under an umbrella, something I loathed in the not so distant past. We also go to the beach after 3 p.m. when the sun has subsided a bit and the rays aren't as strong.

Tip Forty-Four: Light Box in the Winter

Light boxes have been around for decades. SAD or the "Winter Blues" as they are often referred to, has been around even longer. SAD is very common with bipolars. In fact, everyone we know with bipolar disorder has it. When we can't get enough light from the sun, light therapy has been found to be a very effective alternative.

In a recent study: with over 100 SAD patients who used a 10,000 lux system with UV-filtered light diffusion and angular tilt, for 30 minutes each day, about 3/4 showed major improvement of depressive symptoms.

Source: Columbia University Medical Center

The light rays from the box send a signal to the hypothalamus, that part of the human brain that adjusts our inner body clock or circadian rhythm. This stimulates healthy sleep, relaxation, and hormone production, improving health, alertness, and a sense of well-being. Are you thinking what we're thinking? Where do we sign up?

Light boxes compliment your circadian rhythm and the majority of users report it helps their sleep cycle; however, using it too late at night it could disrupt it. The time spent in front of your light box mainly depends upon the light intensity and also the distance between your eyes and the lamp. For example, a 10,000 lux dose of white light for thirty minutes has a similar effect to a 2,500 lux dose for two hours. It is recommended you sit within one to two feet of the box, eyes open; however, not staring directly at the light. Most recommendations are to sit in front of your box once per day; however, some with more severe SAD may need to do it several times per day.

IT'S IMPERATIVE TO TALK TO YOUR DOCTOR BEFORE
YOU TRY LIGHT BOX THERAPY IF:

♦ You have a condition that makes your skin especially sensitive to light, like lupus (SLE).

♦ You take medications that increase your sensitivity to sunlight, such as certain antibiotics, anti-inflammatories or St. John's Wort.

♦ You are feeling manic.

♦ You have an eye condition like glaucoma that makes your eyes vulnerable to light damage.

♦ You have a history of skin cancer.

It is suggested you do not use your light box past 8 p.m. The time of day you do your light therapy is another important factor. Many people with winter depression respond best to treatment first thing in the morning. Some do it in the morning and early evening if they need it more. For people doing shift work, they suggest doing it before their shift begins. This is why it's a treatment customizable for each person and everyone has a slightly different strategy.

Many opt to work at their desk while using it while some people have it by their bedside and use it upon awakening. Others respond better using it in the afternoon. They also have alarm clocks with little light orbs that come on to wake you up. They aren't light boxes, per se, but similar in theory.

It is generally agreed larger boxes with greater surface area are more effective than the smaller ones; however, you can buy and feel relief with smaller, portables ones. There are some which run on batteries and look like little transistor radios and also mini ones that are in long strips designed to fit

> The light box is not approved by the FDA. Some say it is because it is a one-time purchase and therefore less profitable than a new drug.

across your laptop. You can even wear a visor that has it built in with rechargeable batteries! If you Google "light box SAD therapy", you'll see the wide array of light therapy companies and options. Pay attention to the reviews, we cannot stress this enough.

When you're ready to purchase you're light box, several organizations offer help. The Society for Light Treatment and Biological Rhythms (www.websciences.org) offers light therapy guidelines. The Center for Environmental Therapeutics, a non-profit organization formed by doctors and researchers for the advancement of environmental therapies, (www.cet.org) is also very helpful.

It's important to note not all SAD light boxes are created equal. Some are missing very important parts. We almost bought one that had no diffuser! They left it off their spec list and it was only through reading the reviews, one in particular, that we discovered this. Be careful. There are a lot of imposters who won't list all of their specifications and this is where reading the reviews comes in handy. Buying a light box with a diffuser is light box 101. Generally speaking, most of the cheaper ones do not perform as well. The best way to pick one out is to follow the recommended requirements from the C.E.T. and weigh the importance of: size, strength, cost, portability, warranty, shipping and return policy.

LIGHT BOX SUGGESTIONS:

UV Filters:

Fluorescent lamps should have a smooth diffusing screen to filter out harmful ultraviolet (UV) rays.

White Light:

Boxes that emit white light are preferred over blue lamps, which do not provide any known advantage.

Minimized Glare:

In order to minimize glare, the light should be projected downward toward the eyes at an angle.

Lux and Distance:

The box should provide 10,000 lux of illumination at a comfortable sitting distance.

Sufficient Size:

A larger light box is better because even small head movements can take the eyes out of the therapeutic range of the light when a smaller light box is used.

These are recommended requirements by the Center for Environmental Therapeutics (CET).

You may be wondering when you'll feel relief. Improvement can usually be felt within a week or two, sometimes even a few days. It's recommended that you begin before your SAD onset. There are side effects, notably you could get headaches or it could hurt your eyes (especially if you have glaucoma or other eye diseases). One possible side-effect bipolars need to be aware of is potential mania. Most people we read about stated mania didn't last long and they cut back on time in front of their boxes as a solution. Another solution to side-effects could be as simple as changing the angle of your box or moving it further away. Some have two settings and you could also try the lower one. As always, it's suggested you consult with your doctor if you experience any side-effects.

There are light boxes used to treat skin diseases; make sure you are getting a SAD light box. Also, some ophthalmologists have warned that blue light could damage the retina and increase the risk of age-related macular degeneration. So far, there is no definitive research to confirm this; however, it has our attention. For this reason, we did not order a blue light box, based on Honora's degenerative eyesight. If you have any eye disease, consult your doctor.

A good sign is if your light box is approved by the UL, a safety consulting and certification company. It's one of the few companies approved to perform safety testing by Occupational Safety and Health Administration (OSHA).

One final suggestion is pay attention to the warrantees. The good ones will offer it. Most do ten years on the box and two years on the bulbs. We've seen one lifetime guarantee so far, offered by The Sunbox Company; however they still have a return policy that is one month. If you do purchase a light box, we hope it works for you. We wish you less depression, regulated sleep cycles and positive results. Good luck!

 WENDY:

Years ago my psychiatrist sent me off to the medical supply pharmacy with a script for a light box. The nice ladies there opened a catalogue and a large metal box—which looked like an end of the day yard sale reject—stared back at me. I looked at the $400 price tag, was told my insurance wouldn't cover it and thought "oh well, it was a nice thought anyway." As I slunk back into my car seat, I cursed my insurance and ripped up my script.

When I was depressed last year, my psychologist mentioned trying one. I had heard this before. I sat there a bit skeptical, but perked up when she enthusiastically relayed her other patients have had great success with them. I went home and looked online; it was amazing how much the prices have come down!

While researching which light box to buy, we found some excellent testimonials for the Sunbox Company, including a lifetime guarantee. They've also sold them since the 1980's, have been used in many clinical trials, and are made in the USA. We took the plunge, purchased it and began using it yesterday. Stay tuned!

THINGS TO CONSIDER:

- ◆ **Type:** Some light therapy boxes are designed for skin disorders, not SAD.
- ◆ **Light:** Do not stare directly in to the light.
- ◆ **Lumens:** Lower lumens translate into more time in front of your box.
- ◆ **Results:** Results usually take one to two weeks but can be felt in days.
- ◆ **Price:** $100-$200 on average.
- ◆ **Eyes:** Be careful if you have glaucoma or other eye disease.
- ◆ **Color:** White is recommended.
- ◆ **UV:** Look for box that emits less UV light.
- ◆ **Guarantee:** See if the company offers a guarantee on the box and bulbs.

HONORA:

In the past, I used to go tanning everyday. It was unhealthy, but it made me feel good. Or so I thought. Light boxes use filters to remove the harmful UV rays of the sun and tanning beds. I just bought one on Amazon.com and the prices were as low as $50 and as high as $399. Personally, I am always skeptical of the cheap ones; you get what you pay for. Do your research and find the one that matches your needs.

The kelvin (color temperature) is better when it is higher. Five thousand is the highest we have seen, but expensive while four thousand kelvin is average. A woman's comment said her doctor recommended she start light therapy one month before she went downhill. For me, I get depressed near the end of September/early October and it lasts until March.

It's a deep depression that I go through every year without fail. I am really looking forward to trying out a new approach in alleviating my SAD.

> Light Box therapy has been around since the 1980's. The first clinical study was done by the National Institute of Mental Health. More than 2,000 SAD patients have been studied to date.

Tip Forty-Five: Pet Your Pets

Aren't you happiest when snuggling with your pet? What about how they look at you? Often we've felt love in our darkest hours, thanks for our beloved pets sitting next to us, needing us, wanting to be snuggled or walked. It feels like nothing else. Despite knowing that family members and friends love us, sometimes it's the furry ones that get our attention.

In one study, some pet owners experienced an increase of endorphins and dopamine after just 5 minutes with their pets.

•

Pets are powerful forms of stress release, helping lower blood pressure and stress hormones like cortisol, which is associated with depression and anxiety.

It is well documented how our pets reduce our stress. Multiple studies have indicated that they help us reduce anxiety and depression. Pets are also helpful with elevating beneficial hormones like oxytocin, linked to happiness and relaxation.

What if you can't have a pet? How about an aquarium? Watching a fish tank—versus a bare wall—for thirty minutes can lower your blood pressure significantly. The last aquarium we remember was at our annual mammogram appointment. It was so relaxing! We forgot we were in a hospital about to get our breasts smashed. It almost felt like a spa with the robes and our giant fish tank. It looks like we may need to put "buy an aquarium" on our list!

 **WENDY:**

I am a longtime cat owner. They are fun to pet and cuddle with. (Except for my feisty Chazzy, she is another story.) I have enjoyed a lot of love from my kitties over the years. Now Honora has been turned on to the love of cat ownership and understands what I mean. I want an aquarium next. Of course, I don't want to be the one who has to *clean* it. I just want to look at it!

 HONORA:

I grew up with dogs and have always owned one. We had Hagar and he was the sweetest, well-trained golden retriever you'd ever want to meet. He loved to be pet and would be such a comfort to me, to us all. I'll never forget, he was able to carry three tennis balls in his mouth at once! When I graduated college I got Otis, a chocolate lab puppy. He was my best friend, as they say, and gentle with my kids. The perfect family pet. He just passed away last year at seventeen and I miss him dearly. These days we are cat people and very happy. Leo is the hunter, with serious, intense eyes. He climbs trees and is affectionate. He's the man about the complex we live in. He even crawls in to bed with the maintenance man! (Also a cat owner!) Rita was the runt of the littler. She can be timid, but is just a bundle of love, often curled up and purring. I can't imagine my life without them.

What's your pet's name?
Tell us and Tweet us a pic!
@2bipolarchicks

Chapter 10

Attitude Counts: Make It a Positive One

Tip Forty-Six: Accepting Our Illness

In the early days, we thought nothing of acceptance. We were too busy freaking out about our pill bottles, hospital bracelets and how our lives had changed. Acceptance was a blip on the map in distant lands we had no intentions of traveling to. *You want me to accept what?*

Acceptance takes journals filled with ugly entries, endless pharmacy trips, hours and hours of therapy and talking about what you don't want to talk about. The odd thing is acceptance comes when you're not paying attention, much like true love.

> *"Understanding is the first step to acceptance, and only with acceptance can there be recovery."*
> —J.K. ROWLING

Acceptance will not solve your problems like a magic wand. When you are depressed, acceptance will not tap on your psychiatrist's shoulder and whisper the perfect anti-depressant in their ear. When you are manic, acceptance does not put your credit cards on lockdown and deposit cash into your bank account. Acceptance will not pay for your medical care. It is, though, the necessary ingredient to your wellness recipe.

Any person who has this illness and maintains any amount of calm has accepted their diagnosis. You can choose acceptance or you can choose to live in anger or denial; it is up to you. Choosing peace is empowering.

 **WENDY:**

A decade ago, a man once said to me: "Stop playing the victim!" I was so pissed off I wanted to punch him out. (And I am not a violent person.) How dare he? He was a chronically depressed man, like me at the time, and not one to sugarcoat anything. I had to listen though I didn't like what I heard. As his words played over and over in my head, I cursed him less and less and made the decision to not be that girl. I am grateful to him now for opening my eyes to the truth. Did he solve my depression? No way. Did he plant a seed and get me thinking? Absolutely. Today I can distinguish the difference between bipolar disorder as an illness I have versus letting it define all of me. I am grateful I am no longer fighting it or feel like a victim.

When did your

acceptance come?

Are you there yet?

Can you see the road?

> *"Never allow a person to tell you no*
> *who doesn't have the power to say yes."*
> —ELEANOR ROOSEVELT

Tip Forty-Seven: Dream

If you are unhappy where you are, decide where you want to be. Then plot, work, dream, work and plot some more to make it happen. We strongly suggest you find a mentor. They will save you time, money and they'll impart free—free being the key word here—advice. With a mentor, you will always have guidance, someone to bounce ideas off of and get feedback. Instead of guessing, they know from experience.

{
"Never give up on what you really want to do. The person with big dreams is more powerful than one with all the facts."
—ALBERT EINSTEIN
}

Effort is never wasted. From jewelry making to woodworking to dancing to writing, everything takes money and materials, PR and lots and lots of hours of dedication. Have an idea about your timeline and what the costs will be. This is where having a mentor is handy. They can give you reality checks. Often we start new projects in a manic fueled moment or hypomania. But wait. While a spark is necessary, be careful you don't blow it. Make your moves when you are even-keeled. Above all: stay well. You'll want to be healthy so you can enjoy your success and not watch it crumble from the sidelines. We wish you wellness with your success. To do something you love is icing on the cupcake. We believe it is possible for anyone with a well carried out plan and hard work to achieve their dream.

True success for bipolars is to stay alive; but to be alive and fulfilled—that feels amazing!

 WENDY:

It took a long time for me to become a full-time writer. I never liked my jobs and always held them for the paychecks and benefits. I couldn't fathom writing for a living. When I was downsized from my corporate job, I finally had the time and money to start my memoir. However, I was in a suicidal spin, in and out of the hospital so many times I couldn't finish it. When I was in a good place, I began writing again. I waitressed and sold real estate so I could support myself.

When I started to think like an author (even though I was on page thirty of my rough draft), people came in to my life to help me. I found my industry mentor. After plugging away: waiting tables, having two jobs at times, self-publishing, speaking, writing articles, starting the writer's group, making websites, blogging, tweeting and Facebooking, you are now reading our first published book. It was ten years from the start of my rough draft until now. Nothing worthwhile comes easy, but it's possible if you want it badly enough! You have to work hard at staying well first and at your goals, second.

 HONORA:

I was in a deep depression for years and had no dreams. I didn't bother because I thought any month I could be dead. If you made me decide, I would draw a blank. My life had been about my career, my children and then nothing once I lost custody of my children. Then I cared about nothing and dreamt about nothing but seeing them one day. My heart was empty.

Today I am going on with life and starting anew. My present goal is seeing this book to fruition. I never thought I would be a co-author of a book! That was the last thing I thought I'd be doing as a stock broker or Mom.

Tweet us about
your dream and
the climb.
@2bipolarchicks

Tip Forty-Eight: Make a Gratitude List

Making a list of all the things you're grateful for is an instant lift and to see it in black and white helps tremendously. Need a reminder? Going through a difficult time? Have you hit a patch of depression? Write a list and hang that baby where you can see it; perhaps by the coffeemaker, near your bed or on the bathroom mirror. You'll be surprised at all that you have to be grateful for. When you're depressed, it is easy to forget all the things and people in life you have that make life worth living. When you have love and gratitude in your heart, there is little room for negativity.

 WENDY:

Sometimes I'll make them when my attitude is poor or I'm feeling sorry for myself and need to turn it around. My gratitude lists aren't only to help my mood or depression. I make them sporadically and can't believe how much I have to be grateful for. Always at the top of my list: I am alive.

 HONORA:

I have a lot to be grateful for today and making a list puts it all into perspective. I'm amazed when I look at it on paper. I am blessed to have a good family and friends around me. Sometimes, I tend to look at what I don't have and forget to look at my blessings. When I am feeling down, I can forget how good I have it.

WANT TO FEEL GRATEFUL? WHY DON'T YOU TRY:

Gratitude Journal:

Write down what you are grateful for describing what
happened in detail.

Gratitude Letter:

Write a letter to someone, email them, or better yet:
hand-deliver it!

Gratitude Partner:

Regularly share your gratitude with your loved one.

Meditate on the Feeling of Gratitude:

Call to mind things you feel grateful for while meditating.

Express Gratitude:

Thank people during the day for nice things they do.

Tip Forty-Nine: Let Love In

Someone wise once said, "When you can accept love, you will begin to heal." He was right. The trick is how. That is something we cannot teach; it's not found in a book. It is the healing power of love.

Does love cure depression? Unfortunately, not, or there would be no depression or suicide. All the love in the world cannot shield us. However, it can't hurt. Letting love in may mean allowing a friend help you. Or, it could translate into accepting the kind gesture of a stranger. It could be anything. You might understand it once you have weathered the storm. For us, it has sometimes been a close friend or person we are meeting that touches our lives. The trick is to open your heart.

{
"The best and most beautiful things
in this world cannot
be seen or even heard,
but must be felt with the heart."
—HELEN KELLER
}

WENDY:

I was closed off, shut-down for years and didn't know it. From the outside no one guessed as I hid behind smiles and laughter. When I crashed, it was hard to find my smile again. Once I opened myself up, and accepted love from a network of people who cared about me, I blossomed again. Mental illness has definitely hindered me, but it has also brought a special bond of fellow bipolars to me. The list is small, but the company is top-notch.

HONORA:

I have always been very independent. It's difficult for me to let my guard down. I take small steps in this direction. I don't always feel comfortable talking about myself, much less asking for something. It wasn't until I surrounded myself with people like me. Once I felt comfortable enough to open up with a "bipolar friend" I began getting confidence in myself. This, in turn, allowed me the ability to really ask for what I needed. It didn't happen overnight, but it did happen. I don't always practice this; it depends upon how depressed I am. However

I benefit tremendously by asking for help. I invite my friends in to my world. When you invite, you get love in. I try to surround myself with positive people and give back. That's what this life is all about.

Chapter 11

Treatment and Therapies

Tip Fifty: When It's Time to Check In

No one wants to check into the hospital; the door shuts behind you, and you can't escape. Yet, hospitals remain the best solution for bipolars to stay safe and receive immediate relief when in acute manic or suicidal states. Hospitals can bring us down from mania or alleviate our suicidal depression quickly and under close medical supervision. There is no shame to checking in. The problem is we don't want to, especially when we're manic.

Getting a manic bipolar to the hospital can be extremely difficult. It takes an intervention of sorts. We recommend two people joining forces to make sure your beloved bipolar safely and successfully gets admitted. It makes it easier on you.

We have to trust our loved ones and listen if they tell us we need to go. Forget stigma, what your friends, family or job may think. Just get the help you need. Pack a bag, or have someone pack it for you. Whether you realize it or not, the world needs you. They can't have you if you aren't around. It's pretty simple: check-in and stay alive.

 WENDY:

I used to have an aversion to hospitals, especially if I was in a manic episode. Now, I have my "favorite" in the area picked out so Honora knows which one to take me to should I need it. During my last admission in 2006, I felt like a caged lion who had been tranquilized. When depressed, the white walls and fact that you're locked up are so, well, depressing! If you weren't down before you went in, you'll be after! Plus, there's nothing like a plastic, thin, noisy hospital bed to make you appreciate home. It is easy to joke about hospitals—what an easy target—but as time goes by, it's clear hospitals have saved my life. Nothing else matters in the grand scheme. Hospitals can be a necessary, life-saving measure.

 HONORA:

I have been to several hospitals. Not only was I suicidal, but I was also homicidal. I needed serious help! I have had equal times of mania and depression: the crash of mania is earth-shattering. The hospital is the safest place to be when this is happening.

Thankfully, I have not felt the need to check in for a few years now. But if and when the time ever came, I would not hesitate to go. It is a necessary component to any treatment plan and it does save lives, including my own.

IT'S TIME TO CHECK IN WHEN YOU'RE BELOVED BIPOLAR:

- ✦ Is a high risk candidate for suicide.
- ✦ Cannot care for themselves.
- ✦ May be at risk for harming others.
- ✦ Needs to detox from alcohol/drugs.
- ✦ Is not responding to outpatient care.
- ✦ Has become psychotic.
- ✦ Has lost sense of good judgment.

Tip Fifty-One: ECT: It's Electric . . . And Effective!

Electroconvulsive therapy (ECT) has been around since the 1940s. It has a stigma largely due to the early treatments given without anesthesia and its portrayal in Ken Kesey's *One Flew Over The Cuckoo's Nest*. After that movie in the late sixties, treatment dramatically dropped and focus was shifted to medication. Decades later, ECT emerged again, proving itself as a highly successful treatment. Important changes were made such as adding anesthesia and decreasing seizure times. It no longer resembled the dark, inhumane procedure it once was.

Modern day ECT has drastically changed and proves an excellent option for bipolars. The treatment involves inducing a brief seizure—ten or more seconds—while the patient is under general anesthesia. ECT seems to cause changes in brain chemistry that can quickly reduce symptoms of certain mental illnesses. It often works when other treatments are unsuccessful. The average number of treatments ranges from seven to eleven, beginning two to three times a week and tapering off. Patients may go for maintenance treatments, depending upon patient progress and doctor recommendation.

Each year over 100,000 people in the U.S. receive ECT.
It remains the most effective treatment there is, including medication.

ECT IS USED FOR:

♦ Severe, suicidal depression
♦ Treatment-resistant depression
♦ Severe mania
♦ Catatonia
♦ Agitation and aggression with dementia patients

Scientists are not exactly sure how ECT relieves depression. According to the American Psychiatric Association, the percentage of ECT effectiveness is 80%. It is the most effective treatment available.

One thing is for sure: ECT has a proven success rate. It even exceeds medication's effectiveness by up to 15%. Some people are medication resistant or cannot tolerate their medications' side effects. It is a great alternative for these people, too.

As the treatment gets streamlined, the disruption to our lives minimalizes. Fewer treatments are required, most unilaterally, which means less short-term memory loss. Bilateral involves both sides of the brain but are not done as frequently today. This translates to a quicker recovery. In some places—particularly medical suites where you're not

> In a recent study,
> 54% of ECT patients said a trip to the dentist was more distressing.
> 81% said they would agree to have it done again.

in the hospital—you can even stay in your own clothes. From walking in to leaving, you're done in thirty minutes. That's impressive!

If you are severely depressed, manic or your medications are not working, ECT could be an excellent option for you. ECT is like a fine, red wine that keeps improving with age.

 WENDY:

I am proud of the progress they have made with ECT in just the ten years since I have had it done. I feel like an expert in the subject after having many, many ECT treatments from 2003-2004. Today, the seizures are significantly shorter, bilateral (both sides of the brain) treatments are often not needed, and they're administering them outside of hospitals! Wow! It is not, at all, like it was ten years ago.

I had a very close friend who had gotten ECT in the mid-nineties when it was even more rare. I knew it worked well for her and it gave me hope. She had all her long-term memories intact which gave me even more hope. I was desperate, trying to kill myself every few months. I had little choice left. I knew eventually I would die unless I tried ECT so I did.

My friend was bubbly and funny and even made jokes about it. Once when I got lost on the way to her house I had to pull over and call her. I was only two blocks away, yet I couldn't remember those last few turns. When I got there, I was so embarrassed I tried to hide it, but she told me some of the silly things that happened to her. We could relate and that helped a ton. We had a good laugh that day!

All of my long-term memories are intact. This is even despite having many, many bilateral treatments which are thought to cause worse memory loss than unilateral ones.

This is still amazing to me that all my long-term memories are intact, but they are. Thank God! It was a gamble at the time, but I had no other cards in my hand. It was the last one or death. There were two and I did ECT for my family. I didn't care if I lived or died but I knew they did, so I tried it.

Did I lose short-term memories while getting the treatment? Absolutely. But I also wanted to kill myself so I could care less about those days. Forgetting some of the treatment days were a blessing. I wish I forgot more of them.

I absolutely credit ECT with saving my life and would do it again without batting an eyelash. Hands down, it's the most effective treatment there is. Besides going to college, it was best decision I ever made in my life.

 HONORA:

Two years ago I fell into a deep depression. No medication changes were pulling me out of it and ECT was mentioned by my doctor. I knew it had saved Wendy's life, and I was willing to try anything. I gave it a shot and after less than ten treatments the depression lifted. I didn't notice a change until about my sixth or seventh treatment and was just about to give up. My ECT doctor advised me to continue with a few more treatments and I'm glad I did. Some people opt to do maintenance treatments, typically once a month; however, my doctor and I felt it wasn't necessary. It really depends upon the person.

If I needed it, I would do it again in a heartbeat.

Tip Fifty-Two: TMS and rTMS

There have been many breakthrough therapies that are being used, developed and researched. Many are in neurostimulation which involves delivering electric currents or a magnetic field to target specific brain regions. The one being researched the most these days is TMS and rTMS.

TMS, short for transcranial magnetic stimulation, was first used in 1985. It is an up and coming treatment of interest and possible alternative for those who cannot tolerate or do not wish to seek ECT. TMS can be done in an office, with less apparent cognitive impairment; however, recent findings show TMS is the least effective treatment out there.

rTMS, which is a newer form of TMS, stands for repetitive TMS. rTMS involves the application of a rapidly timed variable magnetic field, administered via a coil placed over the scalp, to stimulate brain activity. A high voltage current in the coil generates a focused magnetic field which passes into the brain and induces an electrical field. Applying this stimulation to the left prefrontal cortex increases activity below the stimulation site and produces a reduction in depressive symptoms. Amazingly enough, TMS can currently target sites in the brain to within a few millimeters. We were amazed to hear this.

> Over 400 clinical trials have been done using TMS for: Depression, schizophrenia, anorexia, Alzheimer's disease, autism and cerebral palsy.

TMS therapies, which typically include twenty to thirty sessions, cost between $6,000 and $10,000. As of early 2014, they are not covered by any U.S. insurance that we're aware of.

Our personal verdict is still out since we have not had the therapy ourselves, nor do we know anyone who has. We heard about TMS from our psychiatrist when discussing our options versus ECT; although he wasn't as optimistic about TMS as he was ECT for several reasons: cost and efficacy. Once we heard it wasn't covered by our insurance, and the estimated total cost, we went with our old steady ECT. It is approved and the co-payments were manageable.

There has to be more research, tweaking and results. We remain fans of ECT for its effectiveness, number one, and it's acceptance by insurance companies, number two. We keep a watchful eye on TMS though, as they continue to improve and run trials—increasing its effectiveness—while seeking the stamp from private and public insurance companies.

Tip Fifty-Three: Vagus Nerve Stimulator

The first time we heard about the Vagus Nerve Stimulator (VNS) it reminded us about stimulators used for back pain. As it turns out, it is similar. In 2005, the U.S. Food and Drug Administration approved the VNS for use for treatment resistant depression. They have been used in Canada years before this.

The requirements for approval are twofold. One requires two or more years of depression and the second requires the patient has exhausted four other treatments. It is a last line option since it requires surgery and is permanent.

POSSIBLE VNS SIDE EFFECTS INCLUDE:

♦ Device may come loose, move around or malfunction requiring surgery.

♦ Cough or sore throat.

♦ Voice changes or hoarseness.

♦ Neck pain.

♦ Discomfort or tingling in the area where the device is implanted.

♦ Breathing problems, especially during exercise.

♦ Difficulty swallowing.

VNS works through a device implanted under the skin that sends thirty second electrical pulses through the left vagus nerve, half of a prominent pair of nerves that run from the brainstem through the neck and down to each side of the chest and abdomen. The vagus nerves carry messages from the brain to the body's major organs like the heart, lungs and others to areas of the brain that control mood, sleep, and other functions. This happens approximately every five minutes, which is programmed by the doctor and differs for each person.

It's interesting that VNS was originally developed for epilepsy. Researchers found, as with epileptic meds bipolars often take, it also has effects on mood, especially depressive symptoms.

Although the use of VNS has been endorsed by the American Psychiatric Association, the FDA's approval of it remains controversial. According to a study from the University of Texas Southwestern Medical Center, results of the VNS pilot study showed that 40% of the treated patients displayed at the least a 50% greater improvement in their condition. Most research follows this trend, showing less than 50% effectiveness.

Since the VNS is permanent implant, and has a lower effective rate than other treatments, it is a serious, non-first line choice.

We don't know anyone who has had the treatment; although we look forward to continued progress and improvements as a potential treatment for bipolars.

Tip Fifty-Four: Interpersonal Social Rhythm Therapy

Interpersonal Social Rhythm Therapy (IPSRT) is an effective approach to helping many achieve balance and a reduction in bipolar symptoms and episodes. The therapy—developed by Dr. Ellen Frank and her colleagues at Western Psychiatric Institute & Clinic at the University of Pittsburgh—has gone a step beyond cognitive therapies. While CBT and DBT therapies do involve relationships, social rhythm therapy is a combination of all of them: interpersonal therapy and CBT, with a focus on protecting our fragile circadian rhythms. The fluctuation of any variable within the twenty-four hour day is described as a "circadian" rhythm. IPSRT helps to establish and maintain routines and build healthier relationships. The groundbreaking aspect, in our opinion, is that IPSRT is the only—so far—to have connected all of these dots.

IPSRT integrates some of the scheduling and monitoring techniques of cognitive therapy. It weaves this in with interpersonal problem areas and pharmacotherapy by helping to regularize interpersonal problem areas involving: grief, major life transitions, and our disputes with loved ones, for example. This integration effort includes the new, added regularization of social rhythms, hoping to protect our very fragile circadian rhythms. In a nutshell, IPSRT is the missing link that pulls all therapies we have so far together—and adds protecting our circadian rhythm—in order to avoid episodes.

IPSRT works on resolving relationship issues, keeping our sleep and medication consistent by tracking routines, and reducing stress. The method as outlined by Dr. Ellen Frank, shows specific questions they ask during therapy but also has numeric rating scales. This makes it quantitative and easier to track. It is detailed, using charts, moods and daily living, recording everything from when we wake up to tasks such as having breakfast and first contact with another person. Also, goals—short and long term—and mood charts are used. Another chart breaks it down further to ranges of time for specific tasks such as morning beverage, breakfast, lunch, nap, exercise, dinner, TV and bedtime.

Bipolars have a lot of areas to focus on. We have medication, sleep, stress, relationships and jobs which disturb our mood disorder. Our circadian rhythms are extremely fragile and any pressure or change to them can launch us in to depression or mania quickly. That is why this approach is invaluable as it looks at the big picture. It is a long overdue approach we greatly need.

This is not an illness where we simply swallow pills and that's it. It is one where we have a lot of balls in the air and the wrong rhythm of just one could cause a crash.

Tip Fifty-Five: Dialectical Behavior Therapy

Another popular cognitive therapy is Dialectical Behavior Therapy (DBT) developed by Marsha Linehan in 1985. It is similar to CBT. DBT is often used successfully for people with PTSD, borderline personality disorder, bipolar disorder or any repetitive negative memory or illness. We've had psychologists mention DBT to us. DBT requires first finding a qualified therapist trained specifically to give it.

> DBT was developed primarily for borderline personality disorder and PTSD but has also proved effective for bipolar disorder.

The theory behind DBT is that certain people are prone to react more intensely in certain emotional situations, mainly those found in romantic or family and friend relationships. DBT theory suggests that some people's arousal levels in such situations can increase quicker, go higher and take a longer amount of time to return to baseline levels compared to an average person. This made a lot of sense to us thinking about our own experiences.

The support-oriented method helps you identify your strengths. It is supportive in that it encourages an effort of the family and other loved ones, not just the patient. It's cognitive as it helps change patterns of negative word tracks we say to ourselves. Since depression and bipolar disorder involve negative thinking, DBT is an effective solution. PTSD and/or borderline personality disorder often accompany our illness making us prime candidates for this therapy.

Tip Fifty-Six: Cognitive Behavioral Therapy

Cognitive behavioral therapy (CBT) has been very successful in changing our negative thinking. It works to implement a positive alternative to our negative thinking and experiences.

CBT focuses on examining the relationships between thoughts, feelings and behaviors. Those who receive CBT, in addition to taking medication, have better outcomes than people who do not. In other words, it is not recommended to be a standalone treatment.

In CBT, a therapist encourages the patient to challenge the irrational beliefs they have. They're encouraged to keep track of and write down the thoughts that come in to their minds. These are called "ATs" or "automatic thoughts". The therapist and patient use the log to search and fix negative patterns in their thinking that can cause them to have negative thoughts.

 WENDY:

I can attest to CBTs effectiveness. While at the outpatient Women's Trauma and Addiction program at Princeton House, we did a form of it. (It was done in a group setting which is not the usual way.)

I was in "safety" class. All of us were suicidal, cutters, anorexics or bulimics. In other words, we were in that class until we were deemed safe to ourselves and others. In class, I learned principles of CBT and DBT. It was ten years ago, when I was getting ECT so my memory is fuzzy. I remember we learned about ATs (Automatic Thoughts). It was the first time I even thought about what my thoughts were. *They were horrible!* Once I tuned in to them I realized I needed a lot of work on my thinking.

After my ECT treatments were over, and I was no longer suicidal, I had a chance with this therapy. I give a lot of credit to this class where we intensely worked on our thinking. We recorded our thoughts and examined statements we believed were true. When they were on paper we could look at them more objectively.

It was easier then to separate truth from fiction and detach from the thoughts that I realized weren't true. I saw I was in a fight for my life. I also saw the role my thoughts were playing. It was a war I was fighting. My own, negative mind was against this new infusion of healthy, positive thoughts. CBT was how I won. We also incorporated deep breathing. Our therapists used a combination of techniques and it was very powerful in hindsight.

I have changed tremendously from the girl I was then to now. I understand why CBT is so successful and highly recommend it to anyone.

Chapter 12

BIPOLAR DEFINED

☞ **Bipolar disorder only affects your mood.** *This is not so. It also affects your judgment, concentration, sleep, memory and energy levels.*

☞ **People with bipolar disorder are unable to lead productive, normal lives.** *Living with bipolar disorder can be challenging, but you can successfully work, have a family and stable relationships. The more compliant you are, the easier it is to manage.*

☞ **Medication is the only treatment of bipolar disorder.** *While medication is critical in managing mood swings, there are ways other ways to help. Exercise, sleep, various therapies, minimizing stress, meditation and eating a balanced diet are all proven components to reduce episode severity and frequency.*

☞ **People with bipolar disorder can wish their moods away.** *We wish!*

Tip Fifty-Seven: Getting to Know Us

One of the greatest tips we have for anyone associated with bipolar disorder, including ourselves, is to get educated. This is one way to save lives. Discover how to spot bipolar behaviors and dangers and you can help us, yourselves and the community tremendously. There are many myths about bipolar disorder which cloud the truth about our illness. They add to stigma and prevent many bipolars from receiving treatment. We are a misunderstood animal; ask anyone with the illness and their loved ones. This is common knowledge.

SYMPTOMS OF BIPOLAR DISORDER

- Hyperactivity
- Anger and aggressive behavior
- Impaired judgment
- Increased or decreased sex drive
- Profound sadness
- Grandiosity
- Changes in sleep
- Changes in appetite
- Confusion
- Suicidal thoughts
- Impulsivity (sexual, spending, etc.)
- Pressured Speech

Bipolar disorder is a mental illness that brings severe high and low moods and changes in sleep, energy, thinking, and behavior. The cycles of mood swings can become so severe that it becomes difficult to think or function. These episodes vary in severity and length; some last a day, days, weeks up to months. We've covered them all! To qualify, an episode generally requires a two-week length duration; although rapid cyclers can experience shorter ones and typically experience a minimum of four episodes per year. Ultra rapid cyclers can cycle several times in a day and make up approximately 1% of the bipolar population. As mania and depression pull us to and fro, we do have times of remission—so to speak—where the symptoms of our illness are not as strong.

There is no cure for bipolar disorder; it requires lifelong treatment consisting of medication, using a psychiatrist, psychologist and support. That's the bad news. The good news is that we are creative, charismatic people with higher than average intelligence. Is that the only good news? It doesn't have to be, though it can feel like it at times.

If you look back in history to the famous bipolars, the world praises them and their gifts of music, theatrics, art, literature and innovations. They were not as medicated and treatments were not yet developed. We feel sorrow for our bipolar brothers and sisters of yore for what they had to endure in the early days without modern science. It is hard enough living with it today.

To accept our diagnosis, adjust our lifestyle and battle the addictions that plague 60-75% of us, it often takes a decade or two. Getting to the wellness era takes time. Once we get a handle on the reigns, we can generally have a smoother ride and accomplish stability and life-long goals. No one is bulletproof, but it has been our experience the more compliant we are, the better our lives run.

It is estimated that
2-3% of our population suffer from
bipolar disorder.

It has been reported anywhere from 5.7 to 10 million people in the U. S. are afflicted with bipolar disorder. The reason for the discrepancy—and we believe these numbers will increase over time—is because this estimate is based on those seeking treatment. Many go undiagnosed.

Even in the developed nation of the U.S., approximately half the people with mental illness aren't receiving treatment. Isn't that astounding? We hope as the country improves its health care system changes for the better. We hope the world receives more help too, as we in the U.S. are lucky with regards to health care. As difficult as our health care system can be, there are far too many who have no help at all.

There are other factors besides health care as to why people do not seek help. This could be due to stigma, public perception about mental illness and other reasons, such as denial or unwillingness.

Stigma is a huge problem with bipolar disorder and mental illness in general. Many do not know the truth or seek treatment as a result. A lot of that stems from the media's portrayal of the illness. This could be movies, such as the very old but horrific *One Flew Over the Cuckoo's Nest.* It makes us believe mental illness is to be feared. There are also modern day movies such as *Silver Linings Playbook* which shed a more realistic light, but are only recent. Truer depictions are slowly rolling in. Others highlight mania. Mania makes for a more exciting movie.

MANIC SYMPTOMS:

✓ Restlessness
✓ Irritability
✓ Pressured Speech
✓ Grandiosity
✓ Racing thoughts
✓ Setting unrealistic goals
✓ Excess energy
✓ Hypersexuality
✓ Increased Spending

SYMPTOMS OF DEPRESSION:

✓ Irritability
✓ Crying
✓ Change in appetite
✓ The need for more sleep
✓ Sadness
✓ Loss of interest in regular activities
✓ Thoughts of suicide or death

Since most experts agree bipolar disorder is a genetic illness, looking for clues is critical in early diagnosis within bipolar families. There is bound to be suspicion about someone, based on their behavior, who has yet to be diagnosed. You could very well be right and early intervention is crucial. It is interesting to note bipolar disorder has been known to skip a generation. If this is you, consider yourselves blessed. The next generation will have further medical advancements, treatments, medicine and hopefully less suffering.

The late teens to early twenties are the most common years of diagnosis for bipolar disorder. Few children or young teens—unless displaying extreme symptoms—are diagnosed. This is called early onset and is not as common. Also not as common, is late diagnosis in adults in their forties and fifties. This does happen, though. You can see, there is a wide spectrum in age as bipolar disorder is often puzzling to diagnose.

Bipolars often go under the radar. Here's why. In college, many of us aren't diagnosed until close to graduation. This is often the first time all of the bipolar symptoms collide. Our resulting behavior makes it impossible for those around us to miss. This results in loved ones bringing us to treatment and subsequent diagnosis. We may be exhibiting depression, but hiding it well. This is common for early teens due to hormonal changes. Doctors, if the patient gets that far, are leery to diagnose for this main reason. Many of the symptoms can also be explained by other circumstances.

The same goes for symptoms such as confusion, anger and aggression. What teen do you know of that hasn't experienced these? The feeling could be adjusting, divorce, disliking one's peers, a break up or sexuality issues. Anger could be at a parent, a teacher or friend. Aggression could be a mix of any of these and will come out in any strength. The kicker is they will all hide themselves because no one wants repercussions. No one wants to go for counseling, to the principal's office, go without video games or their cell phones or iPads.

Both of us buried ourselves into sports and activities. We kept peddling and fast. Add to that alcohol and part-time jobs,

> According to the World Health Organization,
> bipolar disorder is the 6th leading cause
> of disability in the world.
> Depression is number one.

our depression went unnoticed. In fact, to this day our parents are shocked we suffered from depression as the façade showed no evidence. People with bipolar disorder make great actors.

No one thinks twice about the first manic episode and therefore no one is prepared. Who is issued the bipolar manual in advance? Unless it is in your family you have no idea what the symptoms are. Even then, it can be missed until the big blowout when all hell breaks loose.

Here's a tip: if it runs in your family, be on the lookout. You'll be more familiar with the behaviors if you have seen them before. Keep a watchful eye as your early intervention may help.

Depression often comes first, especially with female teens. Know enough to take what they say seriously. Never be dismissive. Always talk about feelings and have an ongoing pulse on how they are doing. This is true for any parent, no matter how old your child is. Often, we are the last to recognize our own symptoms. It took us years and years of practice, so having a loved one looking out for us is critical.

For the bipolar: You may feel aggression, mixed with confusion and trouble sleeping. You could be depressed and no one may pick up on it. Or, it may become more apparent. Perhaps your parents take you for therapy. Rarely are conclusions made until the big blowout of the manic episode in your late teens or early twenties. This is easy to see while displayed.

 **WENDY:**

My parents were called down to my college by my roommate. She saw me acting strangely (pacing, talking a mile a minute, not sleeping or eating). I can still remember the looks my roommate gave me, as if she were afraid of me. I had no idea why. When they got there, they were in shock. I had bruises on my arms and legs from not eating and my bank account was overdrawn by five hundred dollars. (Twenty years later, I still thought I was overdrawn by ten dollars until my mom corrected me for this book!)

After years of heavy drinking and pot smoking, culminating in my senior year, I was prime for a major manic episode and diagnosis. My shrink told me it was drug induced, which I took great offense to. (Plus, I thought pot wasn't really a drug at the time.) I remember staying up all night because I had no time for sleep with all my fantastic ideas—though I recall none of them. Food seemed unnecessary. I remember thinking I was fasting or something absurd. At the time, it was spiritual to me. There was no speed other than overdrive. That's mania for you: drive fast 'til you crash.

When I had my major depressive episode in 2003, I couldn't get out of bed. I was told this lasted for six months. I don't remember this. All I remember is countless ECT treatments and being in and out of hospitals for a total of three and a half months inpatient. It was one big blur. I distinctly remember

> Approximately half of the suicides in the
> U.S. are by people with bipolar disorder.

three suicide attempts in great detail and the endless, unshakable feeling of not wanting to live month after month until one year spilled in to the next. I was caught in a riptide, tumbling the majority of the time. I remember not wanting to live, despite the love of my family. Then, because of their love, I felt guilty for not wanting to live. It was a nightmare. I felt the undeniable pain of this illness and a year of treatment that hadn't been working. When this illness has you in its grips, it is a nasty battle.

 HONORA:

I experienced bipolar symptoms for a long time without anyone—least of all myself—knowing exactly what was wrong with me. This is understandable as lack of or misdiagnosis is extremely common with this illness. I remember depression in high school masked by drinking. I had a lot of friends in high school and stuck close to them. That helped. My anger was stuffed inside and then directed at my parents in spurts.

After college, I married my best friend, who was also my drinking partner. As his drinking slowed and he traveled for work, mine continued. With no medication and post-partum, I was a sinking stone. Then I was a revved up nightmare. Finally, help arrived in my mid-thirties with the correct diagnosis and medication. I had a chance at sanity. Until then, I suffered for twenty years without a proper diagnosis and medication. This happens to many people.

Tip Fifty-Eight: Know Your Type

We come in a variety of flavors. From type I to II to cyclo-thalmia to the ones they can't classify, we are all one big family. Our tip is to make sure you know who you are. It's important to know because it will help you streamline your care and give you a direction for wellness.

If you don't have your stamp yet, ask your doctor for it. You need to know this. We couldn't tell you when asked what ours

TYPES OF BIPOLAR DISORDER:

1. Bipolar Type I- Person who has had at least one manic episode in their life. Rapid cycling (at least four episodes per year) falls under this category.

2. Bipolar Type II- Similar to bipolar I, except moods never reach full mania. Instead, one has hypomania – a less severe form of mania—and periods of depression typically lasting longer than periods of hypomania.

3. Cyclothalmia—Episodes of hypomania shift back and forth with mild depression for at least two years. This type is not as extreme as in bipolar disorder I or II.

4. Bipolar Disorder Not Otherwise Specified (BP-NOS)—When a person has symptoms of the illness that don't meet diagnostic criteria for either bipolar I or II. The symptoms may not last long enough or the symptoms are too few to be diagnosed I or II; however, they're clearly out of person's normal range of behavior.

Source: www.nimh.nih.gov and Diagnostic and Statistical Manual of Mental Disorders (DSM-IV) was. Even our parents couldn't. It wasn't until we heard more and more about the Type I's versus Type II's in our thirties that we began to scratch our heads and ask questions. The pieces began to fall in to place. Get your correct bipolar diagnosis so you can discover what makes you different from the others. Just as there are different types of diabetics or cancer sufferers, there are also various types of bipolars.

If you're in the club and you're reading this book, you are one of four types. Let's set aside the Bipolar Not Otherwise Specified (BP-NOS) and cyclothalmics for a moment. (BP-NOS is not in the newer DSM-5 anyway.) If you fall in to one of the main categories: bipolar I and II, there are sub-categories. From there you could be classified as Bipolar I rapid cycling or ultra-rapid cycling for the extra special 1%. To qualify for Bipolar I rapid cycling you must have at least four episodes a year. Ultra-rapid cycling occurs in more women than men, interestingly enough. There is cyclo-thalmia which is the milder form. To qualify, you need at least two years of having hypomanic and depressed episodes.

There you have it: one big happy family of bipolars! Where do you fit in?

 WENDY:

I was diagnosed bipolar I twenty years ago. And what a trip it has been, though thankfully I am clued in to my rhythm now. I also often experience several, marked shifts in mood from hypomania to depression in a year with noticeable behaviors. My moods follow the seasonal patterns of Seasonal Affective Disorder. When the winter comes, I experience depression. When the spring comes, look out! Mania comes to town with it. I've learned my worst depression months are December and January and my most manic months are July and August.

I get mixed in September, October, and May. It makes sense as these are the months when I have attempted suicide.

 HONORA:

I fit into the bipolar I, rapid cycling category. My moods can change very quickly, but I do have a general pattern. It follows Seasonal Affective Disorder as I am consistently depressed in the winter and my mood elevates come spring. Summer is when I tend to alternate between the two, and my mood swings occur quickly. My mania or depression generally doesn't last very long.

> The answer to our manic
> pill-box-company-founder-wannabe?
> Wendy.
> Did you guess right?

Tip Fifty-Nine: Hold On

The ugly truth about bipolar disorder is it takes precious lives. Chances are, if you have this illness, you have either attempted suicide, know someone who has, or have lost a bipolar friend to suicide. It is a grim fact of our illness that one out of five bipolars commit suicide and four out of five try. The statistics spell it out. We beg you to keep communicating your moods.

Suicide becomes more dangerous when we are in a mixed state. This is when we are depressed enough to want to die, and manic enough to have the energy to do it. There is nothing more dangerous than a mixed episode.

Unfortunately, the tendency to withdraw seems built in to us, especially those of us who suffer from extreme depression. The dark thoughts infiltrate and we get in to a place where we feel nothing can change. We are glad we stuck it out and got help. It took us two years of tumbling, but we are living proof you can get through anything and come out the other side.

There is a benefit to holding on. If you weather the storm and stick around, you will feel better. You become tougher. You will know a little more the next time. This won't keep it away like an unwanted telemarketer; you can't simply hang up the phone. (If only it were that easy!) We know it's not. We also know today we are grateful we are having more even days than dark or manic ones.

One in five bipolars commit suicide.

 HONORA:

Depression is crushing. I was in a haze of major depression for a year and a half. There are all levels of depression. Major depression is particularly rough. It lasts. It keeps you pinned to your bed. It is the kind that whispers "take your life. I'm never going away and you don't matter." The kind where your thoughts are running, all towards uselessness and often death, and mental energy is possibly the only energy we have, if at all.

Be careful if you are in a mixed episode. The effort to stay safe is two-fold. One part involves education in advance. The other is communication when you are in the episode which is extremely difficult because our brains are impaired. If your

{
National Suicide Prevention Lifeline
800-273-TALK (8255)
www.suicidepreventionlifeline.org
}

loved ones understand mixed episodes, you will be better off. They will know the signs and get you the help you need if you can't do it yourself. (Which is likely the case.) You can also communicate this to them and/or your doctor. Their knowledge could very well increase your chances of survival.

Please check-in if you have a plan, are feeling suicidal and/or are having dark thoughts. Call your doctor immediately. And keep your family up-to-date on your moods and/or any plans of suicide. Those are alarm bells. This way, you will be able to get an action plan in place.

If you wish to talk to someone anonymously, there are toll-free talk lines for you. Trained and caring individuals are ready to listen to you. Please get help. You are valuable to this world and loved.

 WENDY:

I look back and realize my attempts were always made when I was in a mixed state of depression with a dash of mania. That's when I had the depression to want to die and the energy of mania to carry it out. Suicide and plans were all I thought about. I plotted, attempted and cursed being loved, for that meant people would miss me when I died. I was jealous of the homeless living on the streets of Manhattan. I wanted to disappear in that world too, to be anonymous so no one would miss me. That is how dark suicidal thoughts are. The feeling of hate and self-loathing is immense.

I lied on train tracks. I wanted out! Whether it is by drowning, jumping, trains or slicing our arms, we are hoping for, wanting, betting on death. If we live, it is infuriating to us that anyone presumes to know what was going on in our brains when we attempted. With each failed attempt, I landed in the hospital again.

I looked out many a hospital window wondering when the solution would come. I couldn't understand why the depression wasn't lifting. In hindsight, I was missing the obvious because I was stuck in quicksand: how spared I had been each time my plan didn't work. I am blessed to be alive. People don't survive train tracks. I still can't believe how close I came. None of my dreams of becoming a writer, falling in love, feeling my family's love again in full force and traveling would ever have come true without hanging in there. Sometimes all I did was show up for treatment or consent to be on the flight deck. All I know is I'm glad I held on, despite myself.

Chapter 13

support
yourself

Tip Sixty: Use Outside Resources

We suggest you tap in to all of the outside resources you can. Learn and get connected. Luckily for us, there are numerous resources which can greatly help bipolars and our families understand us. And we need it. NAMI (National Alliance on Mental Illness), DBSA (Depression and Bipolar Support Alliance), IBPF (International Bipolar Foundation) and MHA (Mental Health America) are just a few of the national organizations that can make an enormous difference in our lives. Their national presence is strong, and their efforts to advocate for us are unparalleled. They have excellent websites filled with information and local and state offices providing resources to bipolars everywhere.

NAMI (National Alliance on Mental Illness) is the nation's largest grassroots mental health organization dedicated to building better lives for the millions of Americans affected by mental illness. NAMI advocates for access to services, treatment, support and research and is committed to raise awareness to build a community of hope for all of those in need. Through their popular Helpline, they respond personally to hundreds of thousands of requests each year, providing free referral, information and support— a much-needed lifeline for many.

NAMI uses innovative thinking to ensure that many scientific perspectives are used to advance discovery in the science of brain, behavior, and experience. They look for breakthroughs in science that can become breakthroughs for all people with mental illnesses. In addition, their free twelve and nine-week family and peer programs offer excellent support and education. We also love the ease of their advocacy section.

The DBSA (Depression and Bipolar Support Group) provides hope, help, support, and education to improve the lives of people who have mood disorders. DBSA is primarily a peer-to-peer social network where you can go online and interact with others living with the illness. They offer local meetings and people can start them if there are none in their area. Also, they offer a host of topics in many online discussions.

MHA (Mental Health America), like NAMI, is a non-profit organization that addresses a wide range of mental illnesses nationwide. They work tirelessly to help the mentally ill. The MHA advocate enabling access to behavioral health services for all Americans and have helped shape public policy all over the country.

NIMH (National Institute of Mental Health) is run by the NIH (National Institute of Health). The mission of NIMH is "to transform the understanding and treatment of mental illness through basic and clinical research, paving the way for prevention, recovery and cure." NIMH is the largest scientific research organization dedicated to mental illness in the world! It houses thousands of pulled together research articles and sources free to anyone to access online. You can search on different subjects. We love finding updated bipolar studies on their website!

Another phenomenal organization is The International Bipolar Foundation. Their mission is to "eliminate Bipolar Disorder through the advancement of research; to promote and enhance care and support services; and to erase associated stigma through public education." They have provided many grants, speakers, webinars and advocate strongly for bipolars around the world. They were instrumental in starting the first World Bipolar Day on March 30th 2014.

www.nimh.nih.org
6001 Executive Boulevard
Bethesda, MD 20892
800-969-6642

•

www.nami.org
3803 N. Fairfax Dr., Suite 100
Arlington, VA 22203
(703) 524-7600

•

www.mentalhealthamerica.net
2000 N. Beauregard Street, 6th Floor
Alexandria, VA 22311
(800) 969-6642

•

www.ibpf.org
International Bipolar Foundation
8895 Town Centre Drive, Suite 105-360
San Diego, CA 92122
(858) 764-2496

 WENDY:

I have nothing but gratitude for several organizations and
people involved with my personal support, advocacy, research

and reform. I found that going to local DBSA meetings most helpful when I was suicidal and receiving ECT. I felt self-conscious about my short-term memory loss and they understood me when I felt no one else did. I didn't want to live and they did their best to convince me I had something to live for. I would get out of the hospital (again and again) and they'd welcome me. I will always remember those kind, warm people who helped a lost girl clinging to life.

I also feel indebted to NAMI, MHA and IBPF for their unparalleled and tireless advocacy efforts and support. Many of us are often too depressed (or manic) to take action and these dedicated individuals at NAMI, MHA, DBSA and IBPF literally are our voice.

> www.dbsa.org
> 730 N. Franklin Street, #501
> Chicago, Illinois
> 60654-7225
> (800) 826-3632

 HONORA:

What's great about these websites is most of them offer safe boards to chat and participate with others who share similar experiences and ways of coping with bipolar disorder. There is a lot of support out there with the improvements of online information, forums and blogs. Most require you to open an account. But it doesn't cost a thing. They are all well-organized and professional. You can also set up preferences to your account to receive email alerts to your posts and any articles/ stories you may be interested in.

FAVORITE WEBSITES:

www.PsychCentral.com is the largest and oldest independent mental health social network since 1995. They offer up-to-date information about mental illness as well as over 200 online support groups. They touch the lives of over 4 million people around the world every month.

www.healthyplace.com is the largest consumer mental health site, providing comprehensive, trusted information on psychological disorder and psychiatric medications from both a consumer and expert point of view. There is a social network, mental health news, live mental health videos, live mental health TV and radio show.

www.Healthline.com also offers plenty of useful information. Their main focus, though, is to promote healthy living and ways to manage your illness.

www.BipolarWorld.net is a great site for current news about mental illness. They also have psychiatrists and psychologists who respond to guests' questions about treatment, medications and prognosis. This is a place where families can get help understanding mental illness.

Tip Sixty-One: SSD

If you need help, our tip is to seek financial and medical assistance. Social Security Disability (SSD) has been a lifeline for many of us as bipolar disorder is a very disruptive illness. While it is the hope that we do not need to rely on anyone, government included, this is often not our reality.

{ When you're depressed, completing any
application is overwhelming.
It is always a good idea to get help.
The support alone can get you through it. }

To apply for SSD, go online to their website, www.socialse-curity.gov, and follow instructions. If you need SSD, apply as soon as possible; the process can take years. Part of this tip is not to be ashamed to seek help if you need it.

Getting approved for SSD depends upon the individual person, illness, condition, progress and work history. There is a specific formula you must meet in order to qualify. One year is the required bench mark amount of time at which you would be deemed disabled. There are other specific criteria such as you must have enough work credits. This is determined by your past work history, using a ten-year model. There are exceptions for students.

It takes a long time to receive it if you qualify and the majority of people get denied the first time they apply. You may choose to hire a disability lawyer. They do not collect their fee if they do not win your case. If they do, the government mandates they receive exactly one-third of your lump sum recovery.

There is work on your part. Make sure to gather all medical records and have your doctor fill out his or her part with detailed information about your condition. They will have to fill out details about your illness and a lot of the weight falls upon the assessment of your doctor about your current and past state. There are very specific medical criteria you have to meet. The more applicable records and information you gather, the better chance you have.

 **WENDY:**

I needed help, massive help, to fill out the application in 2003. Fortunately, my mom had a notebook where she had written down the dates of each hospitalization and ECT treatment I had. From this she made a timeline that helped immensely. It took over two years to get approved; luckily, it came when my COBRA benefits, from my previous job, ran out.

I cannot stress enough that if you are still disabled after one year and cannot work: get help and apply. If you're approved, you will receive Medicare benefits two years from the date you applied.

TIPS FOR SOCIAL SECURITY DISABILITY

- Get help with your application (family member, bipolar buddy).
- Hire a disability lawyer to help with your appeal.
- Gather all medical records you can. This takes time so get on it.
- Ask for abstracts of records. Hospitals often charge $1.00/page.
- File after one year of being disabled.
- From start to finish, it takes years. Act fast.
- Bureaucracy is rough. Have patience.
- Find others who have been through the process for support

Tip Sixty-Two: Find Bipolar Buddies

We've learned it's helpful to have a few bipolar buddies who understand our moods, our struggles, lifestyle and inability to always keep plans. They know we have to take care of ourselves and that comes before anything else.

We are very different than our non-mentally ill friends and our families. We could lose our breath daily trying to explain ourselves, whereas we don't have to with our bipolar buddies.

DON'T KNOW ANYONE WITH BIPOLAR?

There are thousands of us online! Try going to popular websites we mentioned earlier. You can meet friends in a monitored, safe environment. You will offer hope and receive it. All for free!

We can say, "I didn't have the energy" and they get it. Or, "I'm too depressed to go." Our mentally ill friends nod their heads and sympathize. We have a secret language, feelings shared and thoughts easily understood. You will never hear a bipolar say, "Just snap out of it."

 WENDY & HONORA:

We have a lot of bipolar buddies. At times they have helped us, at times we have helped them. Our bipolar buddies light up our phones late at night and keep our lives interesting. There is no one who understands us better and we would do anything for them. We can tell within one minute of conversation if they are manic or depressed and vice-versa. We provide rides to hospitals, help on applications and give lots of phone support and love. When someone goes off their meds, we do our best to encourage compliance. When someone is suicidal we offer hope. There is no tighter community and we are grateful for our bipolar buddies.

Tip Sixty-Three: Phone a Friend

Everyone knows phone calls make you feel better. However, reaching out can be difficult, especially in times of depression. We certainly understand depression and it can lead to isolation. However, not only is picking up the phone helpful to you, but you can help the person on the other end of the line. This may prompt you to reach out when you don't want to. Our tip, if phone calls are difficult for you, is to think of who needs you more and pick up the phone to help them.

> *"The best way to cheer yourself up is to try and cheer somebody else up."*
> —MARK TWAIN

 HONORA:

I am a "Chatty Cathy". I love talking on the phone; my cell phone is rarely out of my sight. I have a huge network of friends who I am in constant communication with. Having someone to talk to about the daily grind is therapy for me. My friends know they can call me whenever they need to, day or night. I take great comfort in knowing, not only do I have a great support system, but I can be of help to my friends, too. 3 a.m. phone calls are not unheard of, especially from my bipolar buddies.

Chapter 14

THE END

Tip Sixty-Four: It Will Get Better

Sometimes when we're depressed we feel like it can't get any worse. We're here to remind you just as it can get worse it can—and eventually will—get better. It can be hard to remain positive when your reality is that depression is here and it's not leaving fast enough. It's keeping you from leaving your house, doing things you enjoy and seeing loved ones.

You once smiled, laughed and felt great. When you are severely depressed, borrow someone else's hope. If you want to die, and we've been there, please get help. It will get better again. Depression and mania are inevitable, but fuel up when you are in the middle.

 WENDY:

My uncle used to say, "It can always get worse, Wendells." I hated to hear this and thought at the time, it couldn't. He worked on the floor of the New York Stock Exchange and lived by the daily ups and downs of stocks. It wasn't very comforting to hear, having my uncle remind me of this; although it eventually helped me. After the depression passed I realized the positive side is that it will get better, too. When I get depressed, Honora reminds me of this and is my positive memory.

 HONORA:

Sometimes when I thought I had fallen to my worst, I sunk even lower. I have learned not to think that it can't get any worse. I accept my situation for what it is and know it can always get worse, or better for that matter. I try not to project into the future; I am all about keeping it in the day.

Tip Sixty-Five: The Light at the End of the Tunnel

It's hard to remember there is light at the end of the tunnel. Especially when all we can see or feel is depression. The kind where it's a dark tunnel sloping downwards. It takes people we love to remind us we will get out. When we're depressed and/or suicidal, all we can see or feel is darkness and despair. The ones you love will remind you of hope and light.

 WENDY:

When I was suicidal, remembering I once felt better inside was impossible! Eventually, there it was: the faintest flickering light. I am grateful my suicide attempts failed and I'm alive. Now I'm living my dreams, working full-time as a writer. Who knew life could be so good when ten years ago all I wanted was out? It's that light that my family and friends have to remind me of when I can't see it. It's there. And it will warm me up again like it has before.

Tip Sixty-Six: Have a Little Patience

Often, we're so focused on trying to do everything right, we beat ourselves up when we falter. Not only are there many steps in a day to staying even, but this can be a nasty illness and we must be patient with ourselves.

The big goal here is not avoiding hospitals or med changes or more ECT. The big goal is not trying to be perfect in any or all areas: it is to stay alive. This is our life's mission. When we can boil it down and keep it to this simple mantra—to stay alive—we are better off.

When we beat ourselves up that we have slept too much or under-bathed or not made every planned social event, we have to stop and give ourselves some breathing room. This has been very difficult to do and is a recent breakthrough for us to understand. One of the most liberating things is to realize perfection is not the goal. Ever. In fact, we're becoming aware that it brings on anxiety. And anxiety sucks.

The best remedy is to laugh at ourselves often. Doing things out of our comfort zones helps. The last thing we did was go to karaoke with people we were just meeting. We went a few more times. It was definitely a new thing but highly entertaining. It reminds us not to take ourselves too seriously.

We are like Oscar and Felix in the cleaning department which can drive each other bonkers, ever reminding us it takes patience not solely with our illness, but with each other too. We are not perfect, nor was it ever intended that we should be or strive to be. It is a set up to fail and the amount of anxiety and stress it brings is unhealthy. It can launch even the most level of us into mania. Of course! Trying to be the best we can be takes patience, love and tolerance from ourselves and each other. There is not enough, we find, particularly when it comes from within.

 WENDY:

For so long I focused on doing everything in my power to stay well; however, I left little room for faltering. I got really upset with myself when I was deficient in any one area. I had to—and continue to have to remind myself—perfection is unattainable. It shouldn't be the goal. And if it were, what a boring goal anyway! I wouldn't want to be or meet that person but then why on a daily basis do I often try to be? Not only do I let myself down by expecting too much, life gets overwhelming because who among us can be perfect? It is a dirty word.

 HONORA:

Somewhere along the line I turned in to a perfectionist. Although it is not in every area of my life, I've learned this about myself and I can be a perfectionist in strange ways, especially with my writing, or with something new. The main thing is: I have to give myself permission to make mistakes, learn from it and avoid negative patterns. Next to mania or depression, there is no faster way to summon my anxieties in full-force than to aim too high. It's a hard fall and I fall enough on my own.

ABOUT THE AUTHORS

WENDY K. WILLIAMSON

While studying at Virginia Tech, eight weeks before graduation, Wendy had her first manic episode. It was then that she was diagnosed with bipolar type I. She managed to graduate and worked in a number of fields until being downsized from corporate America. It was then that she plugged in her laptop and wrote her memoir: *I'm Not Crazy Just Bipolar.*

Wendy has written for *BP Magazine, Bipolar Disorder for Dummies: 2nd Edition* and *The Two River Times.* Her book has been reviewed by *Publishers Weekly* and National Alliance on Mental Illness' *The Advocate.* She is the founder of *The Red Bank Writers Group* and has been interviewed on over thirty radio stations. Wendy resides in Monmouth County, NJ, burning out laptops to stay sane.

HONORA ROSE

Honora is a graduate of Boston University. Upon graduation, she worked in the financial industry for ten years before starting a family. She has a fourteen-year-old son and a twelve-year-old daughter. Not long after the birth of her second child, she was diagnosed with bipolar type I. At thirty-five, Honora's years of meteoric highs and crushing lows finally had a name. Her journey to wellness was born.

Today, Honora is co-founder of *The Red Bank Writers Group* and an editor. This is her first publication as an author.

Made in the USA
Monee, IL
24 February 2022